CREATING

VALUE

THROUGH

TECHNOLOGY

CREATING

VALUE

THROUGH

TECHNOLOGY

Discover the tech that can
transform your business

ANDREW HAMPSHIRE

BLOOMSBURY BUSINESS
LONDON · OXFORD · NEW YORK · NEW DELHI · SYDNEY

BLOOMSBURY BUSINESS
Bloomsbury Publishing Plc
50 Bedford Square, London, WC1B 3DP, UK

BLOOMSBURY, BLOOMSBURY BUSINESS and the Diana logo are trademarks
of Bloomsbury Publishing Plc

First published in Great Britain 2020

A catalogue record for this book is available from the British Library

Library of Congress Cataloguing-in-Publication data has been applied for

ISBN: 978-1-4729-6204-1; eBook: 978-1-4729-6202-7

2 4 6 8 10 9 7 5 3 1

Typeset by Deanta Global Publishing Services, Chennai, India
Printed and bound in Great Britain by CPI Group (UK) Ltd, Croydon CR0 4YY

To find out more about our authors and books visit www.bloomsbury.com
and sign up for our newsletters

Contents

1 Background   1

2 Valuation and Value Creation   5

3 Aligning Business Strategy with Technology Strategy   21

4 Technology for Revenue Growth   31
   4.1 Salesforce Management and CRM   33
   4.2 Website and Your Digital Presence   49
   4.3 Marketing Insight and Automation   67
   4.4 Technology as a Product or Product Enhancement 91

5 Technology for Profit Growth   111
   5.1 Digitizing Process   113
   5.2 Business Intelligence   135
   5.3 ERP and PSA   157
   5.4 The Cloud   179
   5.5 Collaboration Technology   199

6 Project Management   219
7 Conclusion   241

Acknowledgements   245
Index   246

1

Background

Advances in technology have arguably had a greater impact on the development of industries and businesses over the past 50 years than any other external force. Technology has the power to disrupt, challenge and transform existing industries along side creating entirely new ones.

Technology advancements are frequent and numerous. There is a constant and relentless pace of innovation that can often leave you with the feeling that the potential shown by one advancement has not even been remotely realized before focus moves on to the next cutting-edge development. Within businesses, those in charge of strategy and in leadership positions such as CEOs, MDs, COOs and board members have varied and demanding jobs and, unsurprisingly, need to spend a great deal of time keeping up with developments in the markets in which they operate, rather than necessarily focusing exclusively on technology. Many conversations I have had with CEOs have been along the lines that they know technology is a huge value opportunity for their business but they simply don't have the level of detailed understanding as to which technologies may be most relevant or the time to keep up with the constant innovation.

Many of them are also scarred from previous investments in IT that perhaps haven't delivered on the value they promised and as such are sceptical that future investment into technology will yield real value.

Therefore, this book is aimed at business leaders, business owners and senior managers who want to develop a meaningful understanding of technology and its real value potential within businesses, and in particular to understand how to apply developments in technology to familiar business principles such as revenues, profit, cash and valuation.

For many business leaders, consistently utilizing technology as a tool for creating meaningful value seems to be elusive and often difficult. There is a typical rhetoric that often describes two distinct and separate groups of people within a company as 'The Business' and 'IT'. It is quite an odd way to divide up a business if you think about it, given how important IT can be to all areas of a business, and its separation in this context highlights the gulf in thinking and understanding that often exists between IT and other senior strategic leadership individuals. If *Men Are from Mars, Women Are from Venus* attempts to highlight (albeit in a light-hearted manner) the generalized difference in communication and thinking between men and women and the issues this can create, then surely there must be an equivalent to describe the gulf between IT and The Business.

How do you overcome this gulf? Some will throw around the cliché that 'communication is key' and the solution is simply for 'IT' to communicate more frequently. This may certainly help, but I think the real key to effective communication is an element of understanding on both sides of the conversation, i.e. both parties understand their own and the other party's position and have the confidence therefore to challenge and question the other side from a position of understanding, not ignorance.

My hope is that through reading this book you will develop a robust framework for assessing technology opportunities within your businesses and the value they may create. I want you to be able to do this with confidence and in order to achieve this, we will construct our framework on robust and familiar foundations – business and financial, rather than technology principles. This is the key to having constructive and valuable conversations between business leaders and IT – if business leaders go into every technology-related conversation at a disadvantage because they feel they need to get into technical concepts, or they don't feel confident in their own understanding of the language and terms the other person is using, it is unlikely to yield positive results.

I am confident that by the end you will have gained an increased level of confidence and interest for technology as a driver of value in the business and most importantly you will have a much clearer understanding of the different ways, depending on your business strategy, in which technology can create value within your business.

Of course in a book like this it's impossible to cover everything, so I've deliberately chosen technologies that are common, applicable to most business environments, and that have the capability to add real demonstrable value to your business. This means there are technologies that I have left out, either because I think there are better opportunities for value creation out there or because there are no clear signs that they are adding value above and beyond a comparable technology. Blockchain is an example of this; it's certainly had a lot of profile and its role in bringing certain cryptocurrencies to life is notable. However, at this point in time I remain unconvinced that Blockchain today, or even in the medium term, is going to be solving problems for businesses that they can't already solve with conventional technologies if they put their minds to it. It's often not the technology that is preventing some of these solutions from materializing, but other factors – politics, competing interests, processes, cost and many other things – that cause the problems. For that reason, I have focused on technologies that solve more pressing problems for most businesses and through which a more demonstrable return on investment will be forthcoming in the short and medium term.

It's also important to note that whilst this book is not aimed at the technology community or technology professionals as its primary audience, it may offer readers in this field some new ideas as to how to frame and position technology with their 'business' colleagues using language more familiar to business leaders.

2

Valuation and Value Creation

Demonstrating the value that a course of action or decision will generate is one of the most basic and universally accepted techniques for successfully asking for something. In any normal business, a request to invest company resources, be those cash or people (or both), will be met with the question: 'Why? What is the business case?'

This is then usually followed by the process of breaking the request down into the associated costs and benefits and then comparing these, taking risks into account, before arriving at a conclusion as to whether an investment makes sense. This is a hugely subjective process and itself often the cause of much of the discontent that surrounds technology investments (see Chapter 6 for an in-depth look at this process).

However, in order for us to talk more plainly throughout this book and ensure we continue to frame our technology assessment framework in terms of business 'value', we need a common and simple understanding of how businesses do create and measure value. For that reason, this book is going to base its concept of value creation around the typical approaches used to value businesses.

It's worth clarifying that I am using a traditional form of value quantification here – namely financial value (and by implication, shareholder value). However, that isn't to say you shouldn't or can't create other kinds of value in a business – either alongside shareholder value or instead of. For example, social value, customer value, environmental value and personal value are all examples of different types of value you can create and no one can argue that one is more appropriate than the other. However, this book is unapologetically focused on shareholder value simply because it is generally what business owners mean when they talk about creating value.

This chapter will look at three of the most common methods used for valuing businesses and break each of them down into their component parts. We will then examine those components to understand the different ways in which technology can impact them.

The three valuation models we are going to look at are the comparable transactions valuation, comparable company analysis and the discount of future cash flows approach.

COMPARABLE TRANSACTIONS

The simplest of valuation methodologies, this tries to put a value on a business using a measure of the business's sustainable earnings and a multiplier based upon previous transactions (acquisitions) of businesses of a similar scale and in a similar sector to your business. Typically used more in private markets, i.e. private equity, it's a relatively simple valuation methodology. The basic formula is to multiply a company's earnings by a number (known as 'the multiple of earnings' or just 'the multiple') and then adjust for any debt or surplus cash that might exist in the business. The formula can be described as:

(Operational Earnings × Multiple) – Net Debt = Shareholder / Equity Value.[1]

More recently, the most frequently used measure of Operational Earnings is 'EBITDA', which is a crude measure of the underlying cash profitability of a company. It is calculated as revenue less cost of sales and overheads and it typically strips out the impact of certain non-cash accounting items (depreciation and amortization), and is stated before tax and interest in order to try and give a true picture of the company's underlying cash profit. In some cases, EBITA is used instead (therefore leaving in the impact of depreciation to take account of continued capital expenditure), but generally in either approach amortization (the 'A') is ignored.

Net debt is effectively the difference between your debt items and your cash balance, and is largely impacted by how much of your profit you can convert into cash.

The multiple is a more subjective figure and slightly more difficult element to quantify. This is where the comparable data comes in. Take a look at the table below:

---

[1]Technically you should be taking out minority interests as well and adding in any financial assets (e.g. investments) that don't contribute towards the operational earnings you've used.

	Share Price	Enterprise Value (EV)	Market Capitalisation	Revenue	EBITDA	Net Profit	EV/Revenue	EV/EBITDA	P/E
CompanyA	£2.50	131,000,000	£125,000,000	£ 24,000,000	£ 10,290,000	£ 5,145,000	5.5	12.7	24.3
Company B	£3.20	156,542,400	£149,542,400	£ 35,000,000	£ 11,500,000	£ 5,750,000	4.5	13.6	26.0
Company C	£5.00	196,500,000	£192,500,000	£ 42,000,000	£ 14,000,333	£ 9,000,000	4.7	14.0	21.4
						AVERAGE	4.9 x	13.5 x	23.9 x

As you can see, there are three comparable transactions with the key metrics set out for EV/Sales (enterprise value/sales ratio), EV/EBITDA and EV/EBITA.

Now, a starting point for a valuation could be simply taking an average of those figures, but that only goes so far. If your company is truly 'average' then that may be a fair approach but inevitably the valuation needs to be adjusted to reflect the value in your particular business. What sort of factors then would cause the multiple applied to move up or down from the average?

The answer is lots of things! The most important factors in determining the multiple are the growth rate, coupled with the predictability of earnings (i.e. consistency). Ultimately, the multiple is a measure of risk and quality – the higher the perceived risk the lower the multiple. The higher the quality (and therefore lower perceived risk) the higher the multiple. As a result there are many other variables that can influence the multiple – factors such as sector, margins (are they high and predictable?), visibility of earnings/levels of recurring revenue, scale, owned IP, brand value, trajectory of earnings, quality of the management team etc. Therefore, whilst this is a more complicated and clearly subjective area of the valuation process, it also offers lots of opportunity to influence the ultimate valuation, and technology can play a valuable role in many of these areas. For example, businesses that are well run operationally with good systems supporting the day-to-day business could be seen as more scalable and with less operational risk, meaning a better multiple can be justified than a comparable business with a less well-developed infrastructure. The reverse is also true. I've seen transactions that start out with a certain valuation at the 'heads of terms' stage (early stage in the process where you agree key points of the deal before getting into diligence) only to have that valuation reduced once diligence has completed because a number of operational and technology issues are uncovered that require a downgrade to price.

Whilst this is a relatively simple valuation approach, there are of course drawbacks to this method:

1 This valuation methodology is most relevant when you are trying to sell or buy a business. It is not that relevant in making business decisions on a day-to-day basis. It gives a clear indication of what a willing buyer is prepared to pay to a willing seller. It doesn't provide an objective measure of value creation;

2 It relies on you finding appropriately similar businesses to compare to;

3 Synergy opportunities may exist for some buyers that are not available to others and this can affect the valuation;

4 The level of competition in a sales process etc.

Key takeaways from the above:

1 The valuation depends largely on either revenue or profit (EBITDA or EBITA) and the multiple adjusted for net cash/debt;

2 All valuation is ultimately derived from cash generation. Revenue, profit, EBITDA, EBITA etc. are all proxies used to try and approximate cash generation;

3 The multiple is a measure of risk and quality and arguably the most subjective area of the methodology.

COMPARABLE COMPANY ANALYSIS (CCA) APPROACH

The comparable valuation methodology is similar in some respects to the comparable transactions approach except that, arguably, it provides you with a more accurate ongoing valuation since there is no 'premium' applied for the acquisition of the business – i.e. your basket of comparable companies doesn't have to have been acquired recently in order that you can use them as a benchmark. This is again a valuation approach that compares certain metrics of a business with a similar business in terms of size and sector to arrive at a valuation, usually using listed companies for which there are daily stock prices to work from and a bigger universe of publicly available data to compare to – the common metrics being EV/Revenue, EV/EBITDA and P/E (price to earnings ratio). It's worth noting here that there is an underlying assumption that public markets are 'efficient' and that the daily share price accurately reflects the valuation. In reality, the smaller the company, the less reliable this is at any point in time. The logic again behind this approach is that all things being equal, businesses of a similar size doing a similar thing should be similarly valued. As such, the starting point for analysts calculating such a valuation will be to determine the peer group – in other words, the companies that your business will be compared with in order to arrive at the comparable valuation metrics.

As an example, consider the table below:

	Share Price	Enterprise Value EV)	Market Capitalisation	Revenue		EBITDA		Net Profit		EV/Revenue	EV/EBITDA	P/E
Company A	£2.50	131,000,000	£125,000,000	£	24,000,000	£	10,290,000	£	5,145,000	5.46	12.73	24.30
Company B	£3.20	156,542,400	£149,542,400	£	35,000,000	£	11,500,000	£	5,750,000	4.47	13.61	26.01
Company C	£5.00	196,500,000	£192,500,000	£	42,000,000	£	14,000,333	£	9,000,000	4.68	14.04	21.39
									AVERAGE	4.87 x	13.46 x	23.9 x

This table shows a small peer group formed of three companies and the key metrics for each one. Generally, an average or median will then form the starting point for a comparable valuation. Depending on the analyst, the sector and purpose of the valuation, it could be that the EV/Revenue ratio is considered more important than EBITA ratio or P/E. This is particularly true in smaller businesses or pre-profit technology companies since it's the only ratio you can run like this and get a vaguely sensible answer.

Regardless of which method you use, you are essentially looking at a small number of components here, once again revenue (sales) and operating profit feature. There is one additional metric not used in private market transactions: P/E.

Price to earnings is essentially comparing the net profit per share (often referred to as earnings per share) with the current share price. It's a very widely used metric with listed companies and is trying to show what investors are willing to pay per £1 of company earnings. For instance, a price to earnings ratio of 25 is telling you that investors are willing to pay £25 for each £1 of profit today. Higher P/E ratios are generally found in businesses that are faster growing and where investors are expecting future share price growth. Conversely, in older, more established companies where share price growth is likely to be slower, you would typically expect to see a lower P/E multiple.

You can see from both of these models that, whether you are looking at private market transaction comparables or listed company comparables, the key measures by which value tends to be benchmarked are revenue, operating profit and a multiple which, as we have discussed, is in part driven by market comparables and in part influenced (positively or negatively!) by the merits or value drags within your particular business.

Briefly, to bring this to life a little, let's pretend we have a business making £2m operating profit (EBITDA) and we will value on a debt-free cash-free basis (i.e. we aren't going to adjust for debt or cash for now – we will simply assume the debt is repaid on acquisition and, likewise, cash taken out of the business).

Taking the first example of a comparable transaction approach, and noting that the average EV/EBITA paid for those deals in the last three years was 8.92x, would suggest a starting valuation of:

$$£2m \text{ EBITDA X } 8.92 = £17.84m$$

Now let's suppose your particular business has a weak second-tier management team and is operationally inefficient compared to other companies, meaning that whoever buys this business is going to need to make investments to fix these issues to avoid slipping too far behind the competition. As a result, you may find the multiple is adjusted during negotiations in order to compensate for that (let's say taken down to 6.5x) and as such your new valuation would be £13m.

Alternatively, let's assume your business actually has a very strong second-tier management team, long-term contracts with customers secured, and you have some unique technology in the business that means you can run the business at better profit margins than your competitor. An acquirer or investor would expect to pay more for this competitive advantage and, as such, you may find the multiple increases to 10x, meaning a £20m valuation.

What you can see from this is that the range of valuations in this case is from £13m to £20m (a big spread) on the same operating profit, the multiple in this case having a big impact on value.

DISCOUNTED FUTURE CASH FLOW (DCF) MODEL

The discounted cash flow model is another common valuation approach. From an academic point of view, this is the only real way to measure value in a business. However, it is notoriously difficult as it relies on forecasts, which are hard to predict, particularly the further out you go. There are a number of varieties of this model, but the principle is simple. You forecast what you think the future cash flows associated with the business are going to be over, say, a 10-year period, then discount them back at a notional rate – usually the company's weighted average cost of capital – to identify the company's value.

This approach is more complicated and involved than the previous two approaches and, unsurprisingly, also requires a lot more data in order to arrive at a valuation. Rather than using history or point-in-time figures to calculate a value, this model is instead forward looking at what the business is likely to generate in cash flows in the future. In order to generate such a value you will need more-detailed information on a business that won't be factored into a comparable valuation approach. For example, a DCF model can take into account changes in strategy, new business lines – things that haven't happened yet – and seek to put a value on them (and pin them down to a specific timing). Arguably, you can get to a more accurate valuation this way, but the output will only be as good as the inputs. It's also a very useful valuation methodology for valuing asset-based investments that don't necessarily have aspirations to grow equity value significantly but throw off cash over a long period of time in a predictable pattern.

Take a look at the example below:

Year	2011	2012	2013	2014	1	2	3	4	5	6	7	8	9	10	T Calcs
		Actuals							**FORECAST**						
Sales	£ 9,000	£ 10,000	£ 11,000	£ 12,000	£ 13,208	£ 13,868	£ 14,631	£ 15,582	£ 16,673	£ 17,840	£ 19,000	£ 20,140	£ 21,147	£ 22,098	£ 22,761
Sales Growth		11%	10%	9.1%	5.0%	5.5%	6.5%	7.0%	7.0%	6.5%	6.0%	5.0%	4.5%	4.0%	3.0%
Net Operating Profit Margin	-8.74%	-16.89%	5.16%	10.15%	15.00%	15.50%	16.00%	16.50%	17.00%	17.50%	18.00%	18.50%	19.00%	19.50%	19.50%
Net Operating Profit After tax	-£ 786	-£ 1,689	£ 568	£ 1,218	£ 1,981	£ 2,150	£ 2,341	£ 2,571	£ 2,834	£ 3,122	£ 3,420	£ 3,726	£ 4,018	£ 4,309	£ 4,438
WACC	8.2%	8.2%			8.2%	8.2%	8.2%	8.2%	8.2%	8.2%	8.2%	8.2%	8.2%	8.2%	8.2%

Long Term Value of Growth	3.0%

FCF model

	1	2	3	4	5	6	7	8	9	10
Change in Net Operating Assets	£ 129	£ 150	£ 186	£ 214	£ 229	£ 227	£ 224	£ 197	£ 187	£ 130
Free Cash Flow (FCF)	£ 1,852	£ 2,000	£ 2,155	£ 2,357	£ 2,606	£ 2,895	£ 3,196	£ 3,528	£ 3,831	£ 4,179
Discounted FCF	£ 1,711	£ 1,707	£ 1,699	£ 1,717	£ 1,754	£ 1,800	£ 1,836	£ 1,873	£ 1,878	£ 39,093

Total Value (Sum of discounted FCF)	£ 55,068

Value Of Business

Total Value	£	55,068
Net Debt	£	667
Value of Equity (value - debt)	£	54,400
Number of shares		300
Price Per Share (£)	£	181.33
Share Price (pence)		18,133

As you can see from the above, you are essentially looking to get to a free cash flow (FCF) figure per year (unlevered FCF) that you can then sum up and discount back to today's value using the weighted average cost of capital. But the free cash flow figure is more of an end result of lots of other factors rather than something you can simply forecast out on its own.

To arrive at the valuation shown, we have to do several things:

1. Forecast out the future revenue projections for the business;
2. Decide how much of that revenue turns into operating profit (i.e. what does that mean for cost base assumptions, profitability by-product etc.);
3. Work out the tax due and as such the NOPAT figure (net operating profit after tax);
4. Decide how much of that operating profit will convert into cash (the 'cash flows') by factoring in other things that use cash, such as capital expenditure, changes to working capital etc. i.e. your net operating assets;
5. Determine the terminal value (the assumption we apply to the final cash flow that provides an ongoing assumption around growth beyond the modelled period);
6. Determine the company's weighted average cost of capital to use as the discount rate to get back to a current valuation.

Whilst distinct from comparative approaches in various ways, in essence you could argue that any multiple-based approach is ultimately trying to approximate a DCF. To that end, you will have noted the similarities – once again revenue and profit both ultimately drive the valuation, albeit forward looking rather than historical. There is also a greater focus on cash conversion in this model, as well as focus on the discount rate used to get back to a present value, something that isn't a feature of the other models.

CHAPTER SUMMARY

What you can see from the above examples is that valuation is a hugely subjective area, although it is based on a very objective ideas, and whilst there are broad parameters and frameworks to work within, many factors influence a valuation. Also, you can't assume that only one valuation approach will be adopted for any given business. Often, two or three different models will be run and the results compared and combined to try and arrive at the most accurate valuation possible.

However, it is clear there are some core fundamental elements common to the valuation models above. Taking these a step further, we can see that value creation is driven by:

1 Growing earnings – either through revenue growth and/or reducing cost/improving profit margins;
2 Generating cash flows that provide returns in excess of the cost of capital deployed to create those cash flows; these cash flows can be redeployed to growth or used to reduce debt, pay dividends etc.; and
3 Increasing the multiple that would be applied to the business (when a multiple of earnings valuation model is used).

It is for this reason that the approach to defining value creation in this book will focus on these key definitions of value drivers and in particular revenue growth, profit growth and cash generation. I will also make reference to the multiple of earnings used in the valuation model, given its importance in two of the three main valuation approaches, and the role that technology can play in influencing this number, both positively and negatively.

3

Aligning Business Strategy with Technology Strategy

SCENE SETTING

This chapter focuses on a core and central concept of this book: the alignment of business and technology strategy. It is essential that the two are interlinked and that one supports the other. This may sound like a statement of the blindingly obvious, but I have been in many businesses that do not have an articulated business strategy (i.e. actually written down and reviewed/shared). I have worked with even more businesses that do not have a technology strategy – again, written down, shared and understood. On that basis, it is an important statement to make, however obvious.

Do you have a clear business strategy? Is it well articulated and is it written down? If I came into your business tomorrow and stopped a member of staff at random and asked them the following three questions, do you think they would know the answers?

1 What are the key objectives for the business this year?
2 What does the business aim to have achieved in the next three years?

3 What is the core unique selling point (USP) for this business that truly sets it apart from competitors?

If the answer is a resounding 'yes' then you are in great shape! If not, then you should think about how you can address this point. Business strategy is a separate subject and not the focus of this book. What we are talking about here is the ability for technology to play a value-adding role in your business, and it stands to reason that if the folks in charge of making the IT strategy happen aren't clear on the answers to the above questions, then it is highly unlikely they will make decisions that deliver on those objectives.

Does that mean you can't add value through technology in this situation? No, of course not – but it does mean there will be a greater requirement on you to direct, review and shape that technology strategy, since only you have the answers to the most important questions needed to make that happen.

The point of discussing value in the previous chapter was to provide us with a common understanding of what we mean by the words 'creating value'. Once you comprehend this, everything else falls into place: different types of technology investments lend themselves better to different parts of the value chain. Understanding this allows you to sense check, challenge or shape a technology strategy based on what you are trying to achieve in the business. For example, if you are seeking revenue growth in your business, you will look to a different set of technologies to support this than if you are looking to cut costs or improve cash generation.

In this book we will look at each value lever (Revenue, Profit, Cash and the Multiple) and the technologies that lend themselves well to creating value. You can then use this as a framework and point of reference when having conversations with your IT managers or when seeking to develop your own technology strategy, in order to ensure that the business strategy aligns with the technology strategy.

Let's now look at a few examples to bring this concept to life and to see how it might work in practice. The first example will show how you can dissect business strategy into its component parts in order to form a new technology strategy from the ground up; in the second example we will look at how you can use the same concepts and tools to assess the merits of a technology strategy that someone else, such as your IT director, might submit to you for budget and your approval.

3.1 WORKED EXAMPLE 1:

Let's say you are the CEO and owner of a business that designs and manufactures electronic gadgets in the UK, selling direct to customers both via your website and over the phone. Let's assume your objectives are:

- To grow the business this year with a self-imposed target of an additional £2m in revenues over and above what you did last year. Let's assume for now that also translates into a proportional increase in profit;
- Let's also suppose you are dealing with some operational challenges in getting your working capital under control as you grow and so you want to reduce working capital by, say, £500k;
- Finally, let's presume you have also set yourself a personal target as a business owner to take some money out in the

next two to four years, and that will allow you to take some money out of the business and bring on a new investment partner in the process.

In summarizing this to your staff, you might explain simply as three objectives:

1 Increase revenues by a further £2m;
2 Improve working capital by £500k;
3 Professionalize and improve the business to make it attractive in the longer term to outside investors.

The key components of this strategy, articulated in the terms we referred to in Chapter 2 previously, are therefore: **Revenue and Profit Growth** – £2m, **Cash Improvement** – £500k, **Valuation Multiple** improvement through the professionalization of the business and reduced reliance on key individuals.

What does this mean for technology strategy?

Firstly, revenue growth of an additional £2m tells us we either need to sell more, charge more, or a combination of the two. You might break that down in the following way:

1 We can raise prices a little, which provides us with, say, £750k of the revenue growth required:
   a. How do you ensure communication of new prices?
   b. How much latitude do individual sales individuals have when setting prices? In other words, how do you enforce the new pricing?
   c. How do you quickly get feedback on the new pricing in case there are any issues?

2 We need to sell more product to the tune of £1.25m sales:
   a. Will this be selling more to existing customers or to new customers?
   b. What does our current prospect-to-order cycle look like and do we have enough in the sales pipeline to deliver £1.25m additional sales?
   c. Will we have to develop new products for this or can we sell our existing products?

Let's now consider what a supporting technology strategy might look like. Well firstly, sales is the focus here so we would be looking at systems that:

- Increase our profile to generate new leads;
- Manage our sales pipeline effectively so the right opportunities are put to the right sales people;
- Control pricing so that sales managers don't apply discounts overzealously;
- Report and track sales-team performance closely so we understand whether we are performing to target.

This might then lead you to conclude that your technology strategy needs a couple of projects that focus on a smart website and associated marketing technologies to drive lead generation. And then a customer relationship management (CRM) platform to manage the opportunities through the sales pipeline and control rules on pricing, alongside providing real-time performance reporting. We also have some idea of how much we can afford to invest in this based on the returns we are targeting, and if we wanted to, we could 'back solve' the required performance improvement in the team to ensure the systems are capable of supporting such improvements.

Cash improvement is the next objective, via a working capital improvement. Since this is a manufacturing business, we could look at reducing inventory, controlling supplier payments or reducing the time it takes to process and receive payments from customers. This might lead you to conclude that the appropriate technology project could be either a warehouse management system that allows for tighter inventory control and better monitoring of stock levels, thus improving the science behind purchasing decisions and reducing stock days. Alternatively, you could conclude that you need a better finance system with more automation in place to chase overdue payments from customers and to prevent early payments to suppliers.

Finally, the objective associated with professionalizing the business and reducing key dependencies might result in you concluding you need a simple but effective HR performance management system to ensure you have the ability to record formal employee development plans and that performance is being tracked across your business in a systematic manner.

All of these are just <u>ideas</u>, and there are many different approaches and answers you could come up with as 'technology responses' to the business objectives. However, in this particular example the technology strategy we are now forming has several clear initiatives: website upgrade, CRM, ERP/warehouse management system, finance system and HR system, all of which directly support the delivery of the business' objectives since that is how they were conceived. At no point in any of this have we been led by trends in technology (although those of course feed into your available solutions); it was borne entirely out of the business strategy, and specifically those levers of revenue and profit growth, cash generation and multiple or P/E enhancement.

3.2 WORKED EXAMPLE 2:

Let's consider the second scenario, in which instead of you coming up with a top-down approach to designing your IT strategy, you are instead approached by your IT manager or a consultant who has some areas in which they wish to invest and is seeking your approval for budget. How could we use the approach above to assess their request in pure business terms and without being dragged into technical conversations?

For the sake of argument, let's assume your IT director or consultant presented the following:

(Note: whilst this example is here to make a point, it is not untypical of the sort of requests you might expect to receive – particularly in smaller businesses.)

- We need to upgrade our file servers as they are ageing and we are running out of disk space;
- Karl from accounts would like to upgrade the finance system as the new one is quicker, has better reporting capability, and the old version goes out of support this year;
- We would like to purchase iPads for the senior members of staff to help us go paperless – it's the way the world is going and we want to be seen to be leading on things like this.

Let's apply the same framework and thought pattern as demonstrated in Example 1 to critically assess and feed back on the above.

We already have our business objectives identified and those won't change. As a reminder:

1 Increase revenues by a further £2m;
2 Improve working capital by £500k;
3 Professionalize and improve the business to make it attractive in the longer term to outside investors.

Working through each of their suggestions in turn, firstly we would ask the IT director which business objectives the upgrade to the infrastructure would support. If he/she said 'the IT infrastructure project will give us the latest server technology and help future proof our IT estate' you might question the rationale, i.e. it's not a bad suggestion but is it a good suggestion with your objectives in mind? However, if they could make a case that this upgrade will reduce the cost of the IT estate and perhaps the personnel costs associated with running it, you might argue that plays to the objective of professionalizing the business, improving profit without the need for revenue growth and improving cash generation through the cost savings.

For the second suggestion you would again ask: how does it support our business goals? They might reply that it will ensure the software remains supported by the vendor and will help finance work more efficiently. In this example, the solution may be right (we also came up with a new finance system in our example above!), but the difference was that the objective for our finance system project was focused on reducing working capital. If you don't give the IT manager (in this example) that same steer, then there is a risk that the project is not orientated around working capital and in itself doesn't deliver on <u>your</u>

objectives (he/she may still be happy, but that's not our priority!). This is a great example of the technology being secondary to the objective – it's the same technical solution we were proposing, but the manner in which you set yourself up to get value from it will be different if working capital is your objective rather than replacing a system that is out of support soon.

Finally, the last suggestion sounds good, and going paperless can be both environmentally friendly and cost efficient. Looking at it with a critical eye, however, you need to identify (in this example) whether that will help bring in revenue or improve your working capital. It may make your business more attractive to acquirers as many investors now are very focused on ESG (environmental, social, governance) factors or sustainable investing and likewise you may have clients demanding you prioritize this. As such you may decide this is a good thing to do and will generate revenue. However, if that wasn't the case you might decide to prioritize other initiatives that contribute more directly to your particular objectives.

I hope you can see that during this appraisal process, despite discussing technologies you may not be confident or familiar with, you are still able to discuss from a position of strength because you are rooting the assessment of this technology in basic business principles – not those that apply to technology.

Now that you have hopefully seen a demonstration of the manner in which this should play out in real life, the next sections will act as a more useful reference point for you as we start to look at examples of technologies that contribute to these different areas of value creation.

SECTION 4

Technology for Revenue Growth

This and the following sections of this book are designed to be a reference manual that you can dip in and out of as required, depending on your focus. In Section 4 and the chapters within it, I have started with the technologies I typically associate with revenue growth; I then move on to those more suited to profit growth in Section 5.

I would suggest you read them through in their entirety to start with and refer back in the future as needed. This first section deals with technologies that can help drive revenue growth. This isn't to say that the technologies we talk about here don't provide other benefits, but that primarily these are the technologies I would be looking at if a business was seeking to grow revenues.

For each technology I will try and provide you with some general context and overview around what that particular technology is capable of doing and the various subcomponents within that. I then look at strategies for creating value with that technology and at some common pitfalls/things to avoid too. Finally, I finish off with one or two case studies for each and a summary at the end. In some cases these case studies are actually several different real life examples, combined and simplified into one in order to help make a point and keep the examples simple.

These chapters will hopefully provide you with a better understanding of a particular technology in a non-technical way and then relate each back to the practical impact it has on the value levers within your business. This isn't going to make you an expert in any of these technologies by any means (most, if not all, of these technologies probably have their own dedicated books if you want the technical nitty-gritty). The real emphasis here is:

a) Awareness – to help you understand what is available, the art of the possible and in what situations it might be relevant;
b) Application to value – how these technologies impact on a firm's value chain;
c) Strategies for getting the most out of the technologies;
d) Bringing this all to life with a few real-life case studies.

4.1

Salesforce Management and CRM

4.1.1 OVERVIEW

Salesforce and customer relationship management systems (CRM) are terms that are often used interchangeably but which in fact represent two quite different systems. Systems aimed at managing the salesforce should be there to monitor and support the performance of the sales team – recording new sales leads, managing a pipeline, tracking sales opportunities as they progress through the sales process, and monitoring the performance of the sales managers themselves. Reporting and analytics in this situation tend to focus on:

- Effort – number of calls made, number of meetings held, how much the sales manager has been able to record about the client and their requirements etc.;
- Outcomes – how many leads are being generated, how quickly they are progressing, win/conversion ratios and so on.

In short, the emphasis here is on the **sales team** itself.

In contrast, CRM systems tend to focus on better understanding the web of relationships a business has with individuals and companies – both customers and prospects alike. Who they are, their needs, how they are connected to you and individuals within your firm – in other words, it has **the customer** as the main point of emphasis.

One of the reasons these two terms are often used interchangeably is because the software platforms that you would use for each system are the same – Salesforce.com, Dynamics CRM, Hubspot, Zoho to name but a few – all of which are capable of doing both. However, the manner in which you configure and use them (crucially, the manner in which you adapt your processes) will differ depending on your focus. That doesn't mean you can't do both, but if you do need to you should do just that – i.e. treat both objectives with equal (and separate) focus and ensure that you understand how the system will be used to perform both sets of tasks. Far too often I have come across businesses that aren't really getting value from their CRM or sales system and it is because of a very generic implementation, which means it is neither a particularly strong salesforce management tool, nor is it a particularly strong relationship management tool. So much of this is down to subtleties in terms of process change, mindset and the way the teams have been trained to use it.

You could use the analogy of football (or soccer) here. Let's say you have 11 players who have never seen or played the game before and you give them all the same equipment – boots, shin pads, a ball, a field to play on and a couple of sets of goal posts and no other direction (no positions to play in, no instructions on how to set up or use the equipment). You will probably find 11 players running around a field kicking the ball, but with little flair or organization and unlikely to display brilliant examples of 'striking', 'goalkeeping' or 'good defending'. Are they playing football? Yes. Is it any good or getting the results desired? Probably not.

Now, this time imagine you split the group of players into two – defenders and strikers. In this scenario you give the strikers very clear instructions that they are to use the equipment to run as fast as possible with the ball towards the opponent's goal and to score as many goals as they can. Then you tell the defenders to use the equipment to try and stop any attacks on their own goal and that they need to spend most of their time based near and protecting their own goal rather than running up the pitch. The result? Probably a superior game, with hopefully better examples of striking and defending. In both examples the equipment is identical. But the implementation of that equipment and the delivery of the instructions to the participants are very different.

4.1.2 HOW TO GET THE MOST OUT OF SALESFORCE AND CRM SYSTEMS

Sales Team Management

With a focus on being very specific about the 'purpose' of the system in mind, let's first look at salesforce management systems.

Salesforce management systems, as noted above, are all about providing your sales director with a system to ensure the sales process(es) are as well managed and optimized as possible. It's hard to improve a sales team and process without good data to work from, and therefore these systems, when used properly, can really help you and your sales director to understand how the sales engine is performing and where additional attention may be required.

The implementations will differ according to your specific business processes, but generally there are consistent areas you will want to focus on for your salesforce system if monitoring and improving the performance of the sales engine is your goal. These are listed below.

Pipeline management

Pipeline management is all about tracking and recording opportunities against a fixed set of pipeline stages. You can then use the data you record to drive insight, help with forecasting and take management decisions. You may have one pipeline or multiple pipelines, but three absolute 'must-haves' are:

1 Unambiguous pipeline stages;
2 The ability to track the dates at which leads go through to the next stage (some systems automatically do this and some don't – so ask the question and plan for it if the system doesn't do this by default);
3 Defining very clear unambiguous rules around what should be recorded as 'The Deal Amount' – for instance, with a multi-year deal that may include services and products, you need to consider whether it is the value of the three years or just the first year you want to record. Making this clear is important in driving consistency within the team and ensuring that you understand what your reports are telling you.

This will allow you to look at things like:

- The number of opportunities by stage, both point in time and same period prior year;
- Average time from lead generation to close (useful for forecasting if you want to understand the likelihood of leads closing in a financial year or quarter; you need to understand typically how long your sales cycle is). It is also helpful to compare this to prior years – is your sales cycle getting longer or shorter?
- In which stage do leads spend the most time before progressing – are these signs of bottlenecks or perhaps not a granular enough set of pipeline stages? You certainly don't want to find that your pipeline stages are too broad and that at each opportunity a long time is spent at each stage. This typically means you won't know that something has gone wrong until it is far too late;
- The relative performance of one individual over another in terms of their ability to generate leads, move things through a pipeline, and their close ratios;
- The number of opportunities at each stage and, come quarter or year end, the likelihood of deals closing based on average closure rates and time taken to close. Finance directors particularly like this one!

Sales engine management
Having the ability to track the performance of individuals within the sales team as well as the team as a whole is very useful. Key features here are the ability to track 'goals/budgets' – both by individual and team – alongside tracking activity levels. You may also

want to integrate this into your phone system – it can provide a number of benefits, from simply providing stats (calls made, average call duration) through to features such as call pooling so that you don't have sales managers waiting for their next appointment. Any unanswered calls from earlier in the day can be pooled and then automatically re-routed to available managers to try them again in between scheduled calls. Taking the above into account, you should then be in a good position to track:

- **Activity levels** – how many calls your team makes a day, who makes the most calls, how this compares with prior month, quarter, year etc.;
- **Outcomes** – the relationship between the number of calls and lead progression through the pipeline, the relationship between call duration and successful outcomes and, crucially, being able to compare individuals in the team against one another using those metrics.

Lead versus opportunity

You will notice that I have so far tended to refer mostly to 'leads', as most people understand the concept. However, most businesses will need to distinguish between a lead and an opportunity and as part of that decide when something moves from being a lead to a fully fledged live opportunity.

Depending on your sales process, the importance of defining leads versus opportunities will vary, but it is something to consider. Essentially, you will need a place in your pipeline to record very early-stage leads – potential sales opportunities that you haven't quantified yet but want a place to log them, versus actual in-flight opportunities, where there is a known and verified sales opportunity and the question is more about whether you are going to win the business rather than whether there is actually a need for your service or product. It is important to get this right since you need your leads to be easy to manage but also completely separate from your opportunities.

Recognizing when a lead becomes an opportunity is also important. If you don't, you run the risk of muddying your pipeline stats and conversion statistics because you aren't starting from the same point each time. To create value from this system you will want to be able to see how your sales engine is performing over time. If you start seeing sales fall, then you want to be able to use this tool to track where and why the conversion rates are worsening as opposed to your own previous best performance (for example, has it got harder to win requests for proposals/RFPs you respond to? Does that indicate a worsening of the quality of RFPs in your business or a new competitor? Have you made new recruits here or changed processes?). This is all very powerful insight but only works if you can trust the data, hence the reason I am making the point about ensuring your opportunities are really opportunities to start with!

CRM

Let's now turn our attention to CRM. With CRM the focus is on the customer and better understanding or serving the customer. Here is the sort of information and the processes you will want to consider.

Basic contact information

Information such as how do you know this person? Who has a relationship with them in your organization? Are they a customer or a prospect? These questions are important to get right; in particular you will want to consider things like, for example, recording multiple contact points against a contact (how often does someone leave a business and then their contacts are arbitrarily 'reassigned' to someone else regardless of whether they know them or not?). This type of information will help with that unless all your points of contact leave at once (but then, of course, you have bigger problems…).

Data that allows you to quantify the total potential value of the relationship
To do this you need to understand the drivers of value from a pricing point of view in your organization. By way of illustration, if you are a software company that prices software on a monthly licence per user model, then you would want to capture the number of employees at each company you speak to and whether they have plans to expand. This is important data to maintain and get right – it's best to have a small number of these fields if you can and ensure that you keep them up to date every time you speak to a customer. If you have too many it becomes too difficult to work into a conversation without it sounding very unnatural and staged.

Information on products they have purchased from you
This should include all products, including any services. Something that works particularly well in CRM systems (yet is seldom done well) is to produce a matrix report showing all your customers down one side and along the top all your products and services, with a tick or cross to indicate whether or not that customer has purchased either of these.

If you can then combine that with the potential opportunity (see previous point on drivers of value), it allows you to be even more targeted with your prioritization. For example, if you are pricing on a 'per employee' basis and your average price is £25 per head per annum, then combining your average price with the number of employees will allow you to size the potential for each company. This isn't a forecast – simply a rough and ready mechanism for prioritizing the relationships you have.

Communication history

Most of us have an expectation that if you call up a company for help or support, it shouldn't matter who you speak to – they should be able to get a picture of your full relationship with the business. Communications logs are crucial here to record all emails, calls and notes on an individual so that whoever is serving the customer can understand the nature of the relationship and prior interactions. As a customer, it is very frustrating to have to repeat yourself.

Built-in customer service processes

Whilst it is rarely done in CRM systems, built-in customer service processes can be very valuable. This means that it doesn't matter who picks up a call or message from a customer or where they are in the world – the customer will still receive the same experience and treatment.

What About Process?

For all of the points above, in conjunction with considering the information that will provide useful management information (MI) and hone the focus of your sales managers, you must consider the business processes by which this information will be maintained and captured. Failure to do this will also result in a less than optimum result (you can see with all these potential failure points we have picked out so far why so many projects fail – there are ample opportunities to do so!).

The first step in considering the process by which this information should be collated is to understand and accept the limitations and constraints you have. For instance, it might sound a brilliant idea to implement a new process that says whenever someone meets a new contact, they enter the information into the CRM system within 24 hours and make a couple of notes on the content of the meeting at the same time. However, if you have a member of staff (let's pretend the MD of an important division) who is allergic to technology and can't use a computer or a phone to save their life, with the best will in the world they are not going to follow this process. Many books and papers on change management will tell you to 'bring him/her on the journey with you' and to 'set the tone at the top', but the reality is that not everyone can get to grips with technology (or change!). Failure to work this limitation or constraint into a process will, again, lead to a failure in the overall implementation of the system.

So how do you get around these limitations? The simplest solution is usually the right one. For example, I have been in a similar situation to the one described above. I worked in a business with a CEO who was brilliant but was never going to use the CRM system – not because he didn't see the value in it, he absolutely did, but because he was just not good with technology. There was no point in extensive training because for that to work it had to be something he would do on a very regular basis, and updating a CRM system isn't usually in the job description of a CEO. Nor was it worth me saying, 'If you don't have the skills to use the system then we will replace you with someone who does', because in reality he was a brilliant CEO and that was more important than being brilliant with technology.

We got around it by agreeing a process whereby he would scribble the job title, purpose of meeting and follow-up date on the back of the business cards and then hand these to his PA, who would transpose that information into the system. The outcome? Decent data going into the CRM system because the process was easy to follow and dealt with the limitations that existed, rather than pretending they didn't exist. Don't go for something that looks good on paper – go for something that works in reality. Easy to say, actually quite hard to do, because you will be concerned with the optics – how will this be perceived within the business? Again taking the example above, when we implemented this process eyes were rolled and people commented that we had spent all this effort implementing a technology solution only to allow someone to take such an 'un-tech' approach to using it. However, it worked well in reality – a fact these same people accepted when they saw the quality of the information that went into the system as a result.

Now this was clearly an appropriate response in that situation – there are of course times where working around something doesn't make sense. For example, if you have a secretary who is fundamentally useless with computers, perhaps it is better to replace them rather than simply 'work around it'. It made sense in the example above because the benefits of doing so outweighed the negatives; the same might not be true in this situation since a large part of the role of a secretary is administration – and therefore IT.

4.1.3 CASE STUDIES

BUSINESS TO CONSUMER (B2C) TRAINING COURSE PROVIDER

This example relates to a B2C business that sold their product (a training course) over the phone. The sales process essentially went like this:

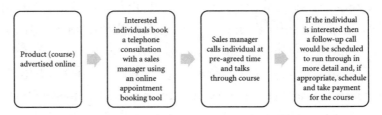

The business was managing this process using spreadsheets in which each day call schedules would be created using a download from the online booking tool and given to each sales manager. Each call was booked in for 30 minutes, and so on a typical nine-to-five day with an hour for lunch and 30 minutes for breaks, each sales manager could have a maximum of 13 calls. Each sales manager would work through their call schedule in Excel and then record next to each one whether they had been successful in booking the follow-up call, selling the course, or whether there had been no response or interest. At the end of the day these spreadsheets were collated, the successful sales sent to the Ops Team for the course on boarding process, and the unanswered calls were combined with the next day's appointments for calling back when possible.

The challenges with the above were:

- MI was variable in quality and certainly not real time, in particular MI on the reasons for lost opportunities were not always clear;
- There were high numbers of unanswered calls, meaning that many sales managers would spend several hours during a day not on the phone as their scheduled call had been unanswered, or ended very quickly, and they had to wait for their next scheduled call;
- Many unanswered calls were 'lost' owing to the very manual nature in which they were recorded and the process for follow-up being organized on a 'best endeavours' basis.

The solution here was to implement a sales management system – the business opted to use Salesforce and in particular focused on:

- Defined pipeline stages that distinguished between 'lead' (first enquiry) and the opportunities as they progressed through a number of calls to a sale;
- Integration with a phone system so that unanswered calls were pooled and then automatically re-routed to a sales manager when available;
- Structured and systemized data capture – to record more information on the individuals enquiring about the product. This helped build up a picture of the individuals most likely to purchase, allowing marketing

to utilize this when marketing the product to a more distinct group of individuals;

- Screens were set up in the office amongst the sales team with information on each sales manager and team in terms of calls that day, calls that month, successful sales, and ranking individuals and teams in real time. This created more of a buzz and competitive sales culture on the floor, which both helped to improve performance and also identify the consistent underperformers and similarly the outperformers.

B2B software vendor

The second case study relates to a company that sold software to legal firms. The business had expanded in the UK and internationally relatively quickly through organic growth and by acquisition. As a result, there were different teams operating in different locations but often dealing with the same law firms (customers). The issue the business faced was a lack of central intelligence on their customer base owing to the acquisitions each bringing their own databases, processes and systems with them.

As a result, there were many instances where customer interaction was not at the level they would expect – for example, where the same representative of the client would have two different conversations with the company because they were speaking to two different teams, which meant neither had sight of the conversation the other team had had and this was causing frustration within the client base.

The business implemented a CRM system in order to provide a master record for all customers and prospects with a focus on recording all interactions with them in one system. The business also decided to embed some of their key client service processes within the system so that common calls and issues were handled in the same way regardless of which team you spoke to or which business the team originally came from. This made a big difference to the customer service levels, with the net promoter score rising from the low 20s to high 80s in a period of a year, and the business winning customer service awards. It also provided revenue growth opportunities as the customer needs were better understood across the business and, as such, opportunities for cross-selling picked up much more quickly. Efficiency savings were also delivered as the business was then able to utilize the international spread to provide 24/7 support to clients without the cost of running teams 24/7 in any location – each location could cover the others owing to the time difference.

CHAPTER SUMMARY

- When seeking to implement a salesforce management or CRM system be clear up front whether you are going to be focusing on the management of the sales team or the client relationship. You can of course do both but treat them as two separate areas of focus.
- For sales team management there are several important areas to ensure you get it right:
  - Pipeline stages – you need to have clear, unambiguous stages and ensure you have the ability to track dates and movement through the pipeline;

- Sales team activities – how do your team currently operate, how do you want them to operate and therefore what are the KPIs you need to focus on tracking in the salesforce systems?
- If appropriate for your business, be clear on definitions of lead versus opportunity and the point at which something becomes a genuine opportunity.

- For CRM implementations, areas it can be helpful to focus on include:
  - The total potential value of the relationship with your customers;
  - The extent of your product relationship with the customer;
  - Your communication history;
  - Customer service processes.

- Be practical when implementing the systems – build processes for the people and business you have – if you accept limitations up front you can design around them. This is often a more successful strategy in the short term than trying to wish them away!

4.2

Website and Your Digital Presence

4.2.1 OVERVIEW

Firstly, a confession. When I first started speaking on the subject of creating value through technology, I was a little apprehensive about including websites in my material. Why? Mainly because websites have been around for a long time, we all know what they are, many brilliant books have been written on the subject, and if technology is meant to evoke a sense of the cutting edge, talking about something that is approximately 30 years old may seem at odds with that. However, websites are the digital gateway to most businesses and deserve huge time and attention to get them right and to make sure the customer receives the best possible experience. As the COVID-19 pandemic demonstrated, websites and digital fulfillment have saved many traditional businesses and increased the share of business conducted online.

Now a question for you. If you were visiting a business with the intention of purchasing something from it and you encountered a chaotic, disorganized office, bins overflowing with rubbish, paint peeling off the walls, flickering lights and old run-down furnishings what would you think? What would you do?

Like many people, I suspect you would turn around and not come back. You certainly wouldn't get the impression that the business was professional, well run or a reputable firm to do business with. Likewise, imagine going to your local supermarket. However, instead of the store looking as it currently does, imagine it has had a makeover. The aisles have all been crammed much closer together and doubled in height, and all signage in the aisles, on the floors and around the store has been removed. After wandering for a few minutes you find yourself in the middle of a tightly packed aisle of goods, shelves all around piled high with a myriad of cans, boxes and packages in a rainbow of different colours, with product names and slogans screaming out from each one. You have no idea which aisles contain which products and you can't see anyone or anything that can help you find your way around. Would you be confused? Almost certainly. Would you have any clue as to which product the store might be drawing your attention to as a potential purchase? None whatsoever, I suspect. You're probably imagining a very complicated scene that is not just overwhelming to the senses but also lacks any form of direction, making it hard to know where to focus.

The purpose of these examples is to demonstrate two things:

1 Visually, first impressions count for a lot. It sounds obvious but we all draw conclusions from our first impressions and so it is important your website visually gives the right impression, one appropriate for your audience;

2 Navigation and direction are important whether you are in a building, in a shop or on a website. If you want someone to take action you need to help them towards that action.

If you would be put off by a reception desk in a business that is messy, overflowing with paper and poorly maintained, or a shop with such a confusing layout you didn't know where to look first, why should an online experience be any different?

Websites are your shop window; they are your first impression and are hugely important, disproportionately so for a smaller business, since the web is a level playing field and you can compete in terms of perception, image and appearance with multi-billion-pound businesses in a way that you couldn't in a traditional bricks and mortar setting.

As I noted in my opening paragraph, websites are not new technology, they have been around since the early 1990s, and for that reason are often not seen as 'cutting edge' or 'technology innovations' (which technically they aren't – they are marketing tools, but you will discover in this chapter that there is much to learn about the technology too). The result? People often overlook the website in favour of bigger, more cutting-edge technology solutions when the payback you get from a well-honed website can be huge.

I like to think of the website as the digital machine that helps a visitor, from awareness through to purchase in the real world. Other technologies that we will cover later on, such as search engine optimization (SEO) and pay-per-click (PPC) advertising, are all designed to attract more people to your website. Therefore, if the 'machine' that is your website is fundamentally broken or not optimized to take someone from awareness to purchase, every pound you spend on those other techniques for drawing more visitors to your site is wasted.

It would be a little like the example in the introduction with the office whose bins were overflowing and paint falling off the walls – that business could certainly spend tens of thousands of pounds on an impressive series of full-page ads in the *Daily Mail* and I suspect it would get people to the door. However, if they were then greeted with that messy reception they would be unlikely to go much further!

For that reason, before you invest too heavily in those other marketing technologies, make sure you have optimized your website as best you can first.

What I hope to give you here is firstly an understanding of the value the website can provide. Then a framework for assessing the opportunities on your website and an understanding of the types of technologies that can help create real value. Finally, some pointers on the sorts of consultants and firms you can work with to take this a step further once you are beyond the basics.

4.2.2 HOW TO GET THE MOST OUT OF YOUR WEBSITE

Let's examine some of the most important principles of websites that I believe will offer you the greatest-value oppor-tunities and, conversely, if you get this wrong, will have a significant and detrimental impact on the effectiveness of your website and hence become a value drag.

Understanding the Role Your Website Plays in Your Customer's Buying Process

The first step in creating real value from the website is to understand the art of the possible in relation to your specific circumstances. That is to say, if you absolutely aced every aspect of your website, what is the best you can hope for? If you are an online retailer then the answer to that question may be simple – your objective would be to see a significant increase in sales via the website. However, plenty of businesses don't complete the sales process online. For example, a restaurant (let's assume not a takeaway for now) may not be selling food online – that takes place when you sit down in the restaurant. Therefore, the objective here would perhaps be to be flooded with bookings, and so you would focus your efforts on that goal. How do you get a website to do that? The website would have to help you stand out, the imagery look warm and inviting; menus need to impress and be easy to access, lots of testimonials from happy diners etc.

Similarly, consider the professional services world. Most companies don't appoint an auditor or consultant online. However, they will use the web to help them find one. Therefore, the opportunity to impact the value chain in that instance would be to stand out against other consultants, ensure your messaging is absolutely honed and it's clear what you do; also, that your imagery and layout presents a high-quality feel and you are positioned as a thought leader in your subject (perhaps thought leadership papers/white papers are made available). In the same way, seamless integration with your CRM system or sales team so that people receive quick responses to any enquiries will be important.

Whilst there are endless scenarios here, the point I hope you can see is that you need to be clear on the areas you need to focus on specific to your customers and their typical purchasing process. You can come at this in a variety of ways. My personal preference is to draw out the buying process and then consider at each stage what role, if any, your website should be playing in that and how you will measure success at the end of it. For illustrative purposes I've set out typical buying processes for a B2C business below and annotated with a few examples of where websites can add value.

Undertaking this exercise is important – if you understand the steps your customers go through in the real world to buy a product like yours it will help you identify how your website can positively influence that from a digital perspective. Out of this should come a few clear areas to focus on and that you can take into all subsequent stages of the process of improving your site.

Intelligent and Informed Design

Intelligent and informed design may sound over-simplified (after all, who would say they were looking for an unintelligent, ill-informed design for their website!), but in this context it means a deliberate, considered design that has had a good process applied to it and has been properly tested (yes, with real people). This means if you are working in a firm that doesn't employ specific user-experience consultants or designers with that skill set then you need to be looking to a third party, which, in case you are wondering, is the case for most businesses.

There are many online companies that will tell you that you can sign up to their online website creation platform and simply use one of their pre-designed templates and be up and running with a website you have designed in minutes. However, if we are talking about value creation here, then we can assume we are looking for an edge over the competitors and therefore it's worth employing specific design skills. (Remember my

Illustrative B2C Purchasing Process

 Identify Need /Problem

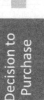 Information Search

 Evaluation of Options

  Decision to Purchase

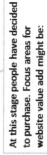 Purchase

Identify Need /Problem

At this stage people will be researching the subject. Therefore focus areas for website value add might be:

- SEO – do you come up top in the web searches for your subject?
- Research/information papers – do you have material on your website likely to inform the individual's research process and explain why your products are superior?
- Is your content clear, concise and in plain English?

Evaluation of Options

At this stage people are narrowing down a product. Focus areas for website value add might be:

- Clear navigation – can people get to the relevant products in very few clicks?
- Clear product specifications, are you displaying the sort of information a consumer might require in order to make a decision and have you called out your strengths?
- Are reviews/evidence of happy customers easy to access?
- Is functionality to compare different models of a product easy to use?

Decision to Purchase

At this stage people have decided to purchase. Focus areas for website value add might be:

- Is it very clear what people need to click to purchase the product?
- Is the checkout process simple or are you asking for too much information?
- Do you have a cart plugin so if someone abandons a shop you can get in touch to find out why?
- Is your cross selling functionality in place and is it intelligent?
- Are you automatically capturing details for the purchaser so you can market in the future (assuming they elect to be contacted)

earlier comments around how the web is a level playing field that enables you to compete with much larger firms if done correctly? Don't pass up that opportunity to look and feel like a bigger business than you are.)

Choosing a third party is often difficult and, like most things in life, recommendations are often worth looking at first given you will have direct access to a customer who can give you insight into their experience and evidence of an end product. However, if you are looking to appraise a third party and don't have an obvious recommendation already, look at RAR (recommended agency ratings) or consider typing UX Agency into Google and looking for firms with case studies or testimonials.

Once you have identified your agency and objectives, you will be ready to begin the design process. A good digital design agency will help you identify your target customers and how many customers represent a good sample – there are even specialist recruitment agencies that can help you recruit individuals representative of your target audience if you struggle to identify specific clients that you could involve. Clearly, if you can involve your own clients then that is obviously preferable.

The trick here is to iterate the designs frequently, in small incremental steps, and seek feedback from a sample/client group regularly (not the same group each time). Typically, design will follow a series of stages, the first being sketches, followed by wireframes, possibly followed by a prototype before the final versions are then created. It is important you follow these stages as a little time spent on this up front can save a huge amount of costly rework later on if designs are not correct. At all times you are evaluating the design of the site against your objectives. If it doesn't hit the objectives – don't spend time on it.

For existing websites you will typically start with user-experience testing before commencing any redesign work at all. For new sites this is usually done at the prototype stage. It is again something often done by a specialist – most digital design agencies offer this and there are also a number of dedicated user-experience consultancies that just provide user-experience testing. This type of testing often involves filming the sample of individuals using your website unaided so that you can see where they hit issues.

By way of illustration, I am aware of an online retailer that went through this process a number of years ago as their website sales were lower than they should have been. When they filmed a user operating the site, they watched as the user became more and more frustrated clicking the 'add to basket' button but with nothing happening. After some time they gave up trying to purchase the item. Interestingly, the user's perception was that the website wasn't working – in fact they had added the same product to their basket more than 10 times but because nothing happened on the site to tell them, they didn't realize they had. A simple user-experience alteration of creating a message saying 'added to basket' once the button had been clicked rectified this issue and had a positive knock-on impact on sales. It's very hard to get this sort of feedback without testing in this manner because if you simply ask the users why they aren't purchasing they would simply say it is because the site isn't working. Cue lots of developers picking apart the code base to work out why the code isn't firing as designed. The user wasn't capable of articulating the real problem – hence the value that this sort of testing can provide.

Other things to consider within the design process are the extent to which you are featuring 'calls to action', i.e. points on a webpage that are asking the user to do something – register, contact us, download a demo, download a white paper, subscribe to marketing updates. Many websites again make the assumption that as long as contact information is available on the website, users will find it if they need it. Sometimes users don't know what they need and a little encouragement from you in terms of a 'next step' for them to take, such as registering for a webinar etc., is all that's required. (Think about how you nudge them along to the next stage of that purchasing process, which we looked at earlier).

Content
This is not a guide on writing styles nor is it a marketing manual; however, it would be remiss to talk about adding value from a website and not mention content. Firstly, it's worth keeping in mind that websites are not read. By that I mean most people scan websites quickly rather than read them. Research has shown that in fact most people read in patterns. For example this could mean scanning pages in an 'F' or 'Z' shaped pattern, that is either two horizontal lines and vertically or starting top left to top right, diagonal down to bottom left, then across to the right again. It can also mean scanning pages to read headings or bold sections. This has many implications but for content it means several things:

1 Getting to the point in as few words as possible is critical;
2 Ensuring that the visual design of the site makes key words and phrases stand out (go back to your customer's

purchasing process to help you figure out what those should be) so that you break the scanning process and encourage the website visitor to read;

3 Key design elements should be built around the typical reading patterns and there should be a flow to the design.

Whilst of course you want to spend time wordsmithing a website, in practice few visitors will truly appreciate your efforts! Less is more and one strategy can be to focus on putting wordy information into separate downloadable files rather than on the main body of websites. You also need to think about SEO (more on that in a minute) and the influence your content may have on search engine rankings. Typically, the more relevant content you have on a subject, the better you will perform in SEO rankings. This doesn't necessarily mean you need huge volumes of content – you can focus on one or two key messages and build your content around those themes. That can also mean structuring your content around questions, as this is how people generally carry out searches. If your website doesn't have a FAQ section, for example, then you are missing a really simple trick for getting your messages across in a way that aligns with the sorts of questions your potential customers may be asking.

SEO and PPC

Search engine optimization (SEO) and pay-per-click (PPC) are two strategies for bringing more people to your website. Whilst the end objective for both of these is similar, i.e. attempting to obtain the highest possible ranking on the front page of a search engine's results page, they are very different.

The primary difference is that SEO is centred around understanding the manner in which search engines work, the manner in which people search for your type of product or service, and then optimizing your website both creatively and technically in order to ensure the search engine ranks your website ahead of a competitor's site. Pay-per-click, on the other hand, is a more straightforward pay-to-win style approach, where you pay each time someone clicks on your advert; the amount you bid for the keyword determines where you appear in the paid search results ranking. Often, SEO is seen as the first place to start as it is perceived to be 'free' (but isn't really) whereas pay-per-click has a specific financial cost per visitor. I say that SEO isn't really free because whilst there is no explicit link between a click and a financial payment in the case of SEO, the work involved to optimize your site for SEO, and remain optimized and ahead of competitors, can be demanding and certainly not free if you think about the staff, time and even third parties that can be involved in this process.

Understand how search engines work
It's important to understand how search engines work when ranking your pages if you want to optimize your site for SEO. This is a complicated subject and one worth engaging a specialist firm to carry out, but I shall attempt to highlight some of the more important features to take note of. It's also worth saying that there are literally thousands of excellent resources on this subject, from books to videos, podcasts and websites, and most search engines also provide their own guidelines.

Firstly, remember that, like your business, search engine businesses are also trying to offer a unique service to their clients, and in the search business that means serving up webpages to Internet users that are most relevant to the question they are trying to answer. If a user searches for something on Google and they get an answer quickly and it is the right answer, then it stands to reason the next time they have a question they will go back to Google. In the same way, if a user were to search on Google repeatedly and never really find what they were looking for, they might try a different search engine. The important point to keep in mind, therefore, is that these firms are constantly looking at their search algorithm with a view to ensuring it returns the best possible answer (the highest quality and most relevant) for any given question from one of their customers. Whilst the way in which the algorithms do this is complicated, broadly speaking they carry out two tasks:

1 Crawling and indexing – this is the process by which a search engine will programmatically 'read' your website, catalogue what it finds so it can then attempt to score the relevance of your site to the question being asked;
2 Assessing quality – in general, search engines use links back to your website as a proxy for quality. If you have other high-quality sites referring and linking to yours, the search engine will deem the quality to be higher than a site that doesn't.

It's worth mentioning search engine algorithms change all the time and as such staying on top of this is harder than you think.

Understand how your potential customers work

Alongside understanding how the search engine algorithms work, the other key component is understanding how your potential customers work – or more specifically, how they are likely to search for your product or service. You have to know which keywords and search terms will optimize your site. This is a combination of understanding the problems that your product solves, the search terms and questions that relate to those, and then it's a delicate balance of narrowing down to something that is specific enough that you direct genuinely useful traffic (audience) to your website but not so specific that there is simply no traffic for that keyword. Tools like SEMrush or Google's keyword tools will help you with this.

Optimize the visible AND invisible

Once you understand how the search engines work and you know what keywords and phrases you are looking to optimize, you are then into the process of optimizing. Some of this is visible on the website (content, layout etc.) and some is invisible.

Visible aspects to consider include clear titles, well-formed content that is optimized for keywords, ensuring the pages are easily shareable, and so on.

The invisible aspects relate to the metadata on your page (think of this as the descriptions and additional information you attach to your content that can be read by the search engines but not necessarily seen by the user). Examples include a clear site map (help those robots understand your site layout), content tagged appropriately with HTML tags, alternative text for images, the 'meta description' for your website etc. Google provides a comprehensive guide on optimizing your site for their engine and this is worth a read. As at time of print you can access that at the following link: https://support.google.com/webmasters/answer/7451184?hl=en

Measure, adjust, repeat

SEO is a continuous cycle of action, measurement, review and repetition in order to continue to stay ahead of your competitors. It's certainly a hugely valuable area to focus on and worth working with specialists – remember, this isn't meant to be a 'how to' for SEO so that you can do this yourself but more a guide to what it is, to demonstrate the value but also the complexity of this area and therefore convince you to spend time and expert resources on it.

Extensions and Integrations

There are many forms of plugins and technology extensions available for your website. These vary in quality and practicality, but I think a couple worth calling out are shopping cart abandonment plugins and integration to CRM and Salesforce systems.

Firstly, shopping cart abandonment – we've all done it, carefully assessed the product we want to purchase, added to the cart, began the checkout process and then, for whatever reason, failed to complete the purchase. The opportunity here for your business therefore is to ensure you have a technology solution on your website that is capable of identifying these abandoned carts and can help automate the follow-up email prompts to those individuals in order to encourage them to complete the purchase.

CRM and Salesforce systems are covered in Chapter 4.1, but integrating them with a website is a useful way of ensuring leads are not lost and that you have as few barriers between an enquiry and follow-up as possible. Integration can take many forms; at its simplest level it can be a 'contact us' form on your website that then creates a lead in the CRM or Salesforce system to be followed up by a team member. However, it can also be more complex – if you capture a little more information from the individual submitting the form you can score or profile the lead and send out one of several automated responses designed to help them along the purchasing process.

4.2.3 CASE STUDY

AN AIRLINE SEEKING TO OPTIMIZE THE PURCHASE PROCESS

This case study is a good example of several of the themes in this chapter – the importance of user-centred design, the value of real world testing and just a hint of caution when seeking to make things too brilliant! This particular business is an airline and their objective for this project was to try and make it as simple as possible to book a flight. They had gone so far as to set a specific time goal of 60 seconds for how quickly they wanted someone to be able to go from start to finish to book a flight on their website. The project involved various design phases, input and feedback from a sample customer group, and demonstrated many of the good practices we have talked about. However, in an early version of the website, when testing for real with the sample client group, many of the customers were in fact very unhappy with the site. The reason? In an attempt to make the purchase process as simple and seamless as possible, the airline had removed too many steps from the booking process and as a result, individuals who thought they were browsing for flights had actually booked them instead! The testing process picked this up and allowed the design team to make the necessary adjustments. It's a good example of how even with the best intentions and clear objectives, until you test for real with a group of representative customers, you can never really know if your design is going to hit the mark.

4.2.4 CHAPTER SUMMARY

- Websites are not a new concept and have been around for a long time. If you ask people to talk about cutting-edge technology most will not include websites (and to a certain point they would be correct).
- However, websites offer huge value potential to businesses and therefore it is a technology you should be assessing and improving on a regular basis.
- The web is more of a level playing field than bricks and mortar and you can look and feel like a bigger and more sophisticated business than you could do in a physical setting.
- The first priority when seeking to create real value is to understand the customer buying process and overlay how your website can impact on that. This will ensure your design decisions tie back to optimizing and improving a clear source of value – i.e. a sale.
- Design is an art and a science – utilize expertise here and spend more time than you think on this part, as a good

design is the difference between achieving your objectives and not.

- It is important to focus on content – consider the relationship between the words you write and the design/the way they are presented.
- Start with improving the machine that is your website before you spend too much money bringing more people to it. However, when you are ready to do that…
- SEO and PPC are strategies that can increase traffic to your website, as is social media, which we will look at in the next chapter.

4.3

Marketing Insight and Automation

4.3.1 OVERVIEW

Marketing technology has evolved significantly over the past decade or so and the sheer number of products you can subscribe to or purchase that promise to help you improve your marketing efforts is enormous. This chapter will focus on a few areas of marketing technology that I think are particularly interesting and offer real opportunity to drive revenue improvement in your business. These are:

1 Understanding what customers or potential customers really think about your brand, business, products and services;

2 Understanding how you can better target the types of individuals your products and services are most applicable to;

3 Acting upon that insight through automation and smart use of technology to ensure no lead or opportunity is missed, you maximize your ROI, and that you deliver a consistent high-quality sales experience.

There are different technologies you can utilize to help you achieve the above. I still see a number of businesses that start with the technology and then work their business into it. This can result in having too many technologies trying to work together. As with all chapters in this book, we will start with the business problems and work out how we combine technologies to solve them. Let's explore each of the points above and within that look at what we mean and what sorts of technologies you can turn to for help. We'll then address how you get the most out of them.

Tools to Help You Understand What Customers Think and Say
About Your Business, Brand or Products
It's very hard to improve or optimize something if you don't have a clear view of what you have to start with. In this particular case we are talking about marketing and therefore if you want to improve your marketing – whether that is getting a better return on investment for your marketing spend, better lead conversion, shortening the sales cycle or simply reaching more potential customers – you need to be clear on who your product is aimed at, how you currently go about targeting those individuals and, in parallel, whether there are things about your product or business that would prevent you from successfully selling to those targets.

Social listening is a great example of technology that has fundamentally changed the way certain aspects of businesses can operate. Consider a business, say, 15 years ago that wanted to understand what people thought about their business or product. The typical solutions to that problem were things like customer surveys – either on the phone or in the street, focus groups, market research, product testing etc.

I recall one evening, as a 16 year old, doing some shopping in Canterbury after school one day and being stopped by a firm in the street who were conducting research and feedback for a producer of crisps (potato chips to my friends outside the UK). We were offered £10 to sit in a room for 30 minutes and literally eat hundreds of crisps and provide feedback on each one along with our views on a few different crisp brands. (It was as tasty as it sounds – I did enquire at the time as to what one would have to do in order to turn this experience into a full-time job, but to my dismay professional crisp tester is not a recognized profession!)

The point of the story is that back then, to get real and reflective feedback about your product and service you had to invest time, effort and bodies in getting hold of the data, and since individuals knew they were providing feedback it was perhaps not always the most honest it could have been. I was 16 and had been given both money and crisps – I was in a pretty good mood as a result and unlikely to seriously insult my benefactors!

Social listening has changed that quite considerably. Instead of sending out surveys or armies of people, because of the more public and online way in which people now express their thoughts and feelings, it is much easier to get feedback and comments directly through social media than ever before. Arguably, in many cases the feedback is also likely to be a little more honest, simply on the basis that on most occasions people aren't posting it to be used as feedback – they are just expressing a thought or opinion (not always the case, of course).

Social-listening tools essentially analyse and pull together insight from across social media platforms in order to present you with trends and information about your brand. They typically look for mentions of your brand or product in posts, use natural language processing (NLP) and similar technologies in order to analyse sentiment and then use the metadata associated with those posts to help you aggregate and analyse by, say, geography, demographic, date and time etc. Some of these tools are designed in order to help you identify issues and then catch and respond to them quickly. Others seek to use the same technology but to provide analytics and trends rather than necessarily encouraging a real-time response. Some of the big platforms – Brandwatch, for example – cover a range of capabilities from sentiment analysis, real-time response and analytics to help you understand more about your audience. For instance, what are the other things your audience are typically interested in? Who are the influencers in your space whom you could be collaborating with? Ultimately, the more you understand about your audience, the more effectively you can design a marketing strategy that is personalized, segmented and more likely to succeed. It's also helpful to understand the sentiment around your product or service – if feeling towards your brand is good, then great – what do people like and how do you keep doing that? Likewise, if sentiment is poor, what insight can you glean from that and how can you act upon it? Perhaps worst of all is if there is very little out there at all about your business, i.e. no sentiment, which may be an indication you need to do more to promote and market your brand or bring it closer to the forefront of people's minds.

Building upon social-listening tools, as I describe later, there are firms you can work with that own proprietary databases and tools that allow for far greater insight and analysis on social media, with a greater focus on richness of analysis and predictive capability than necessarily on real-time stats or action. These databases have often been built up over many years and allow you to not only analyse the data in far greater detail but also understand trends, and with a greater volume of data. Many of these firms have data science services and teams built around them, meaning that if you have specific questions you would like answered with the data – particularly in terms of any relationships that might exist or how you can use the past insight to help predict the future – they can provide you with the expertise to do this.

Of course, social media is not the only place to go for feedback. For example, good old-fashioned contact forms on websites, if properly configured, can offer insight into sentiment and feedback from clients directly. By the same token, website review sites and aggregators of that sort of data can provide valuable insight into what people think about your product and service.

These sorts of tools aren't for everyone, and clearly the more you interact with large groups of individuals in a public way the better. That is to say, retail businesses will get the most value from this type of analysis, businesses that sell to a large client base, whether Business to Consumer (B2C) or Business to Business (B2B), probably come next, and ultimately businesses that sell niche product and services to a small number of businesses are unlikely to benefit as much. For example, a business manufacturing engine parts for an aerospace firm are unlikely to gather as much insight from such practices as, say, a clothing retailer. However, that isn't to say there isn't value to be had here, albeit you may end up needing to focus any analysis on trade forums, niche bulletin boards, emails to customer services (don't forget those – they are important and can you honestly say you properly analyse those at the moment?) or perhaps business-focused media such as LinkedIn rather than, say, Twitter or Facebook for your insight.

Tools to Help You Understand How You Can Better Target the Types of Individuals Your Products and Services Are Most Applicable To
How do you target clients at the moment? Email, social media? Traditional mail?

Do you analyse performance of these, response rates, impact on web traffic, follow-up? Do you analyse open and click rates etc.?

In an ideal world, every email or marketing message you put out there would be opened and read by someone who connected with the message and then went on to buy your product and service. Of course that is impossible to achieve, but the objective is to get as close to your target audience as you possibly can with each marketing campaign and to use insight and learning from each to improve targeting on the next. Thankfully, there are plenty of tools that can help you do this.

Some of these tools provide data on specific targets; others provide feedback on how you are doing on connecting with targets you have already identified. Both are useful and certainly not mutually exclusive.

Starting with insight on your existing campaigns, most marketing automation platforms will provide you with feedback on engagement rates, be that via email campaigns, text, social media and other forms of marketing. Again, most will provide you with information such as the split between desktop and mobile use, time of day analytics, and many go further to then recommend times of day and days of the week on which to send the campaigns to get you the best engagement rate.

I mentioned Brandwatch earlier as an example of a tool that can provide better insight into your audience. Others such as Hubspot or various Salesforce add-ons that are more focused at marketing automation and inbound marketing are very comprehensive when it comes to insight into marketing campaigns and suggestions for improvements.

Using inbound marketing technology is another area to consider – the concept here being that rather than pushing messages about your business to customers, you create things of value to them that draw them to you and generate leads that way. For example, white papers, thought pieces, free eBooks, blogs, online articles (all with a link back to your website or some other online presence) are all examples of areas that can be used to drive inbound leads. Using a technology platform to help you manage this and create a co-ordinated and joined-up campaign across different types of content and channels can be helpful in ensuring there is a coherence to what you are doing, alongside providing you with useful MI on the effectiveness of these campaigns.

There are other ways of course to gain insight into your target market. Firstly, in the case of businesses targeting individuals, social media again can provide an insight into your target market. The level of targeting you can get to on platforms such as Facebook (individuals) or LinkedIn (businesses) is impressive and, if nothing else, using these tools to understand the size or other interests of your target market can be insightful.

In the case of businesses targeting other businesses, there are a number of tools out there that collate data on businesses – usually from a single golden source such as an online company register like Companies House in the UK and Dun & Bradstreet in the US – and then add to this with their own proprietary insights and data. This could be email addresses or contact information for individuals at the firms, more information about the companies themselves (sector, employees etc.), news flow, all of which can help you better understand your audience if properly utilized. Dun & Bradstreet are one of the better-known providers of such data and I've seen good examples of this put to use to help map markets. To give an instance, if you are selling cleaning services to businesses in London, wouldn't it be great if you could quickly size the opportunity by pulling together a list of all companies in London that were serviced office owners or operators. You might then quickly organize the data by size of firm or specific geographic areas and then use that to form the basis of a more targeted and considered marketing campaign.

If you look hard enough you may find there are very specific insight tools for your particular market. By way of example, I recall many years ago working with a business that sold services to the government and local authorities. We found that there was a tool designed specifically for businesses like that which allowed them to see exactly how much was spent by each government department and local council and with which firm. The tool then went even further to provide insight on upcoming tenders by utilizing minutes from council meetings and other committee meetings that suggested when a potential procurement exercise was imminent. This was great insight to feed into the business development teams. The purpose of this example is not that it is going to be relevant for every business, but that if you look hard enough you may find some very niche data services aimed specifically at your industry, and making use of these could make a lot of sense if you are looking for an edge over your competitor or simply to increase the sophistication with which you understand your market and the opportunity available.

Tools to Help You Act Upon Insight Through Marketing Automation Platforms

If you don't already use it, a marketing automation platform would be a good place to start. Marketing automation systems are designed to combine the typical elements of digital marketing into a single platform and focus on driving efficiency and automation into the process. The objective of these systems is to create leads that you can then move through your sales funnel and close. Typically, when people think of automation they think of standardization and mass repetition of the same thing, hence a temptation to see this sort of marketing as less sophisticated or personal. This is, however, incorrect. The power of an automated marketing tool is significant and can ensure lots of the little details that make for good sales practice or customer service don't get overlooked. Typically, these platforms combine email, social media, online marketing, website integration and reporting/analytics. There is also usually an element of CRM built into them or they come with integrations to common CRM systems alongside elements of workflow and logic.

In terms of email marketing, these tools will allow you to do the basics you would expect – segment audiences, send out marketing emails and track the results. However, they also offer greater levels of sophistication. For example, a number of these tools will allow you to do A/B testing and send different versions of an email to different groups to see which design is more effective. Some platforms like Hubspot can take that a step further and send out a smaller batch of emails first, use the stats to see which version of the email was more effective and then send the most effective email to the remainder of your marketing list. Similarly, email automation is a key feature of these tools – automating a 'thank you, we will get back to you' when someone emails your customer services team, automating follow-ups when people express an interest in a campaign etc. Say you send out an email advertising a particular product or promotion. You might automate a follow-up email to go out three days later to anyone who clicked on the link but didn't complete a purchase to prompt them to get in contact if they would like to discuss it. Support for email scheduling is common in order that large email campaigns can be sent at various times throughout the day/week/month in batches to allow you to more easily manage the inbound enquiries and alter your strategy based on the initial stats.

Social media capability in these tools generally focuses on combining activity across multiple social platforms into one system, making it easier to manage. As with the email campaigns, expect a level of analytics and insight to help you refine your approach as well as things like scheduled posting, targeted messages and social listening, as described earlier. As you will know, with social media one of the challenges is posting frequently enough to keep people interested whilst managing the workload of a busy marketing team. Using a platform to perhaps upload a week's worth of content at a time and then scheduling for release across multiple channels throughout the week can be a real time saver and ensure nothing gets missed.

Marketing automation platforms usually come with a database you can use to record leads, prospects and customer information (a bit like CRM) in order to improve analytics and allow you to build up a better picture of interactions with an individual over time. This allows you to undertake activities like email or social personalization – and even something as simple as seeing in one system that John Smith first came to your business via a specific marketing campaign, has visited specific pages on your website, has read white papers or articles, and has visited your social media sites several times helps you build up a much better understanding of him as an individual when you then utilize more traditional marketing approaches (such as a phone call or conversation!).

Since these platforms are designed to generate leads, lead scoring is a common feature of marketing automation systems. You will typically get to set the parameters that go into a lead score and then allow the system to track scores for each individual you interact with so you can prioritize those with the highest scores.

Reporting and insight/analytics is another core component of these systems. By integrating these various aspects of marketing, you end up with a data-rich environment and it is then up to you to use that data to gain insight into your processes and database and subsequently take action.

Integration with and management of SEO and paid advertising is another typical area these tools focus on. There are of course plenty of tools, such as those you get with Google, that allow you to do this; however, there is value in being able to manage this from one place and to combine with the rest of the data and insight you are getting across your marketing channels and platform. Likewise, landing-page builders and data-capture forms are simple to manage from tools such as this and integrate with data in the rest of the platform (CRM, for example).

Going beyond marketing automation platforms, there are other neat technologies out there that can help you take action to improve the precision of your marketing. For example, consider incorporating geo-data/location information into your marketing. This could be as simple as focusing your online advertising to specific geographic regions or providing different messages depending on which region a search or prospect is based in. Other tools can be more real time and interactive – tools like Fluid Ads will help you design campaigns that are triggered when individuals enter a specific physical location. This could be near a shop, a particular area on a map or some other location-based trigger that allows you to then provide very specific targeted ads. Perhaps information on a product you have in-store or an offer for a product, should they interact with the advert. This is an aspect of marketing automation that offers far greater potential than is currently utilized by the majority of businesses.

4.3.2 HOW TO CREATE VALUE WITH INSIGHT AND AUTOMATION TECHNOLOGY

Be Realistic and Identify Your Goals

This will start to sound like a recurring theme in this book, but, after all, we are trying to bring together an understanding of technology's ability to create tangible shareholder value with your business's own specific value levers. If that is our goal in the business you run/work in, then this should also be the first question you ask yourself – how can this help me add value to the business?

Firstly, understand your existing level of sophistication. If your business already utilizes many of the technologies and techniques outlined in this chapter, chances are you are in good shape. If that is the case and you are also happy with the performance of your marketing machine, then many congratulations – you can probably skip to the next chapter. If you aren't happy either because you believe things can be improved or that you do none of this at the moment, this is important to understand so that you can set realistic goals. If you are such a firm, you can make some pretty big leaps just doing the basics. Your goals might be based around seeing an increase in social followers, email engagement or website traffic.

If, however, you have many of these tools but for whatever reason aren't getting the value you expect from them, then your goals may be more focused on specific areas you need to improve first – you might need to spend more time A/B testing your content or reviewing the way it is written if it isn't working in order to improve click rates or your ability to move leads through the funnel.

Ultimately, you need to determine what effect digital marketing can have on your sales cycle, in other words, you need to be realistic. This is covered in part in Chapter 4.2, but you should think about this here too. For example, an online retailer would say the best outcome from a good digital marketing campaign is a conversion of leads to customers, i.e. making a sale(s). Conversely, the business we saw earlier, making engine parts, might determine that brand awareness amongst the professional community that they will be selling into is the ultimate goal here, to feature more frequently in the minds of those individuals responsible for procuring engine parts from companies like theirs. Therefore, tracking the extent to which their marketing is hitting the right notes with the prospects, the extent to which their content is being read and interacted with, and then subsequently using that to personalize follow-up content would be good use of the technology.

Think about how well you understand perception of your brand and products in the market and, similarly, do you have a good handle on those questions with regards to your closest competitors? If the answer is not very well or not as well as you would like, then one objective may be to better track and monitor this more closely in order to inform new product development and save cash and investment in unnecessary R&D.

There are numerous other questions you can ask yourself here, but the important thing is to set goals that are a) realistic and b) track back to the way in which your business makes money. Understanding your sales cycle and customer journey(s) is the first step, then how either greater insight into these customers or how automation could improve the sales pitch to them can be utilized.

As an example of taking action before doing some proper thinking, I once knew of a B2B cleaning services firm who decided to spend a lot of time and effort on building a Twitter following. Why? Because Twitter was new and cool and everyone was doing it… The problem was it was indiscriminate when targeting individuals, and posts were literally about cleaning. The result was a lot of time and effort wasted as the majority of the individuals who stumbled across this account were not the target audience and the cleaning business put little effort into anything other than continuing to post without segmentation or any real objective. (What was the best they were hoping was going to happen?)

Build Your Data Over Time – Don't Buy It

This is probably going to make me very unpopular with list sellers, but the reality is that through a combination of just common sense and GDPR regulations in the UK and Europe, it doesn't make a huge amount of sense to buy your databases. You want to spend your time interacting and communicating as much as possible with people who fit your target customer and who are interested in your firm and/or your products. Whilst it can feel great sending an email campaign to thousands of people, if most of those are wrong for your business or they would never buy your product (and perhaps have no idea you even have their data), you can generate a lot of negative feeling pretty quickly.

You will find building up your database yourself – utilizing techniques described here (and in many excellent marketing books), will in time leave you with a far more valuable store of data than anything you could purchase.

Get Specific and Personal (...within reason!)

These tools are, in part, about providing you with the insight and intelligence you need to optimize and hone your marketing approach. You are a skilled surgeon wielding your marketing scalpel, not a crazed lunatic wielding a chainsaw. The power of these tools is to segment your data, and not only segment it but think hard about the ways in which you want to interact with prospects digitally in order to maximize your chances of generating business from them. You will do this by targeting carefully, spending time understanding what the data is telling you – whether that is segmenting it by specific characteristics or perhaps being more targeted in your content strategy and who you send what type of information to. This is where the power of these tools comes into play.

Personalizing content is also a great way of doing this; use integrations with your CRM system to help personalize content. For instance, don't run the risk of sending someone an email telling them about a product if there is a chance they have already purchased it. Utilize the power of the data you have and personalize wherever possible. If you know they have purchased men's clothes in the sale from you before then send them an email the next time you have men's clothes on sale!

Landing pages are another example of this. If you are going to send out a campaign telling people about a great new autumn line-up you have or a specific product you are featuring, have them land on a page specifically focused on that when they click the link in the email. Why? People are going to click on a link if they are interested in something they have read, therefore taking them to a page that removes all other distractions and focuses them as simply as possible on whatever message you are trying to get across and <u>whatever action you want them to take</u> is important. It's also important to distinguish landing pages as a result of a PPC campaign versus an email campaign. In the case of PPC you need to make sure that your landing page aligns with the search term someone is using to find your PPC advert. We've all experienced the frustration of searching for something and then having to search again on a website to find it. For example, if you search for 'custom T-shirt printing' and click on a link that promises this, but then the page you are taken to is a general page about clothing or garments, you are going to be frustrated as you've then got to hunt around until you find what you thought you were going to be taken to when clicking the link. These are the little details that make all the difference.

Think About Integrations

As you can see, these systems are built around data – either as an input or as a useful output. As such, it is important you are able to get data in and out of these systems. Don't take it for granted that this is easy to do – even well established systems can surprise you with their lack of reporting capability or ability to integrate easily. I cover this more in the Business Intelligence chapter (5.2), but when choosing a system do spend time looking at the systems that the platform can integrate without the box. Whilst in theory it's possible with APIs to get data in and out of most things, you don't want to waste time messing around with various third-party tools just to get hold of your data.

For example, if you know you need to integrate with your CRM system and your CRM system happens to be Salesforce, then look for marketing automation systems that will integrate with Salesforce to save you time and stress later on. Likewise, if you already have a reporting database or data warehouse, spend some time up front with your technical team making sure they can get data out of whatever system you are looking at into the format you need. Most of these tools have example APIs with test data you can use and you don't usually have to purchase the product to work with these. You don't need to be an expert in any of this – just keep in mind it needs to be done and so make sure you tee up someone in your technical team to have these sorts of conversations before you commit. Whilst not exhaustive, the sorts of integrations you would expect to see from a good marketing automation platform would be:

- CRM
- PPC
- Social media
- Website
- Traditional media – TV, bulletin boards etc.
- Online directories

Spend Some Time Lead Scoring
As noted already, these systems are here to help you create leads and therefore it's worth spending some time understanding the lead-scoring capability within these systems. Each of them works slightly differently but the concepts are the same. You can set various parameters and events within the system that are designed to either add or subtract points from a particular lead. These scores are applied to each record in the system and allow you to identify the most-relevant leads. For example, let's say you are selling a software product online aimed at businesses that need to manage their expenses. You might set up a lead scoring and choose to award or deduct points as follows:

+ 1 point for visiting the website
+ 1 point for visiting the website more than once in a day

+ 1 point for clicking on a link in a marketing email

+ 1 point if their job title is COO, CTO, CIO or CFO

+ 2 points for registering to download your white paper on expenses management

+ 3 points for clicking on the 'request a demo now' link

And…

− 1 point for taking no action after receiving 2 or more marketing emails

− 1 point if the section of the website visited is a careers/jobs page

− 3 points if the email address matches the domain of a competitor

Obviously these are just examples and the key to getting real value from this is to iterate and develop this over time. Each time a lead is flagged as a high-scoring prospect you should ask yourself whether it is right to have been flagged as a high score and if not why not − where have you gone wrong in configuring your lead scoring? Perhaps not differentiating between meaningful events and more trivial events in your points-scoring system is a good place to start looking.

Work Closely With the Sales Team
This may sound like an obvious point but it is important to have good alignment between sales and marketing. In many businesses there are different teams doing marketing and sales and thus you need to make sure there are mechanisms and processes in place to provide ongoing communication between

the two. For example, you don't want your marvellous automation system emailing leads with early-stage email campaigns if your sales teams are already having detailed conversations with them. It looks unprofessional and can be pretty annoying if you are on the receiving end. Likewise, when nurturing new leads think about the point in the process you hand off to your sales team – don't try and automate all leads to a close! Do enough to get them into the process and interested and then it's a combination of sales and marketing as required to get the prospect over the line.

4.3.3 CASE STUDIES

SOFTWARE BUSINESS USING DATA TO SIZE A MARKET

This first case study is a good example of using some pretty simple data to provide useful insight into a sales process.

I worked with a software business many years ago that sold administration software. They had a relatively simple pricing model that priced their software as a service (SaaS) on a per head basis along with some professional services fees. Therefore, if you knew the headcount in any given business, you could calculate what the software was going to cost.

One of their challenges was that pretty much every business in the world needs administration software and so in theory their 'end customer' was every business in the world! They needed to cut this down and focus on specific segments in order to build up credibility and track record in specific areas of the market. However, they didn't want to do this opportunistically or by accident and then inadvertently find they ended up specializing in what could turn out to be a very small market.

We worked with them to utilize a standard Dun & Bradstreet style data set and on a company-by-company basis worked out the potential sale for each business based on headcount and a proxy for professional services. We then grouped those businesses using SIC (sector) codes and that told us pretty quickly which segments of the market were the largest potential segments. We then overlaid their existing customer base and the resulting Venn diagram showed us the segments that were largest and that they had credible expertise they could sell into. The result was that they could then build industry-specific marketing collateral, case studies and campaigns, and use that to generate new leads rather than targeting the market in a very generic manner.

RETAIL BUSINESS USING MARKETING AUTOMATION TO IMPROVE LEAD GENERATION

This second case study features a retail business utilizing marketing automation to aggregate data from across website, social and email channels in order to better inform their marketing strategy. The firm first used this data to understand the types of content people were engaging with and the types of content they weren't. This then fed into a round of email campaigns, with content seen to be more attractive to prospects. These email campaigns featured a variety of products and services and the resulting analytics from those campaigns then allowed them to segment their data-base based on which link in the email (related to a specific product or service) the individuals clicked. The result was an increase in engagement with email campaigns and an increase in inbound enquires to the sales team for follow-up conversations.

4.3.4 CHAPTER SUMMARY

- There are a large number of marketing technology plat-forms out there that can help you refine your marketing strategy.
- Distinguish between the need for insight and the need to take action – it may be the same system does both, but you will need to use them deliberately and separately to undertake this if you want to get maximum value from them.
- Social-listening tools and social-analytic databases are great ways of understanding what people think about your brand, product or business.
- Some of these tools are designed to help you identify the emergence of an issue or crisis and respond to it there and then; others are better at providing more long-term analytics to help inform strategy.
- If you spend time looking into the analytic capabilities, you can learn a lot about your target audience, their related interests and how you might more effectively target them.
- B2B businesses can also benefit from data sets that provide insight into a market or industry segment, rather than just focusing on individuals.

- Marketing automation tools are very useful in helping you manage key aspects of your digital marketing strategy in one place.
- Owing to the number of software products you can purchase in these areas, being really clear on your customer journeys, and what role you want digital marketing to play in those, is critical before embarking on a project. Otherwise you run the risk that the objective is to implement the system rather than whatever business goal you actually want to achieve.

4.4

Technology as a Product or Product Enhancement

4.4.1 OVERVIEW

Much of the focus of this book is on how you can utilize technology to support your existing business – i.e. reduce costs, improve efficiency or drive additional revenue to your existing products and services. However, it would be remiss of me to write a book about creating value with technology without at least one chapter that focuses on the role technology can play as the product itself. Now for those of you running a technology business already, this chapter is unlikely to be particularly relevant – this is a subject that can fill a book on its own and the chances are this is an area in which you will already be doing plenty of thinking. However, for those of you who don't run a technology business and don't think you will ever run such a business, this may just give you a few ideas as to how you might develop or repackage some of your existing assets into a digital revenue stream.

There are a number of reasons you might consider looking at technology as a product or product enhancement. Typically these are:

1 You have an asset you have decided that you can utilize in a digital way to create a new revenue stream (e.g. proprietary software, a unique and valuable data set etc.);
2 Your competitors are doing it and you need to compete;
3 The market you are in is fundamentally changing as a result of technology and therefore your business will cease to exist in the future in the way it does now.

These are deliberately ordered in a way that illustrates the control you have over the process and therefore the urgency with which you would approach this. If you have an asset you believe you can monetize digitally, then the onus is on you to figure that out, and the time and cost you invest in that is determined by you, presumably based on the expected return. If you are responding to the actions of a competitor, then you have less of a choice as to whether to do it, but within reason you can still control the timetable – particularly if you are using the time to come up with a differentiated offering.

The last point is the more challenging to deal with and you often have little input into the decision to transition your business model or the timetable. An example might be within the music retail industry – shops that sold CDs and cassettes had their industry fundamentally altered with the advent of digital music players and streaming services. Not only had the format become digital, but the model itself (i.e. the concept of purchasing albums) was changing to more of a rental model with streaming services such as Spotify. Interestingly, niche retailers – for example those specializing in rare records or vinyl – seem to have struggled less with this since their audience are after an experience rather than just access to a song or album. This may also explain in part why some booksellers continue to survive long after the introduction of e-books; many readers enjoy building a book collection and prefer the 'feel' of real books to electronic books – they are after an experience greater than mere access to the content.

When considering technology as a product, you will need to assess whether the product is there to directly generate revenue, or to support a revenue-generating product. By that I mean, are you monetizing the technology directly such as charging some to use, say, your in-house developed software? Or are you providing it to make your other products more attractive/provide a competitive advantage?

So what are the areas you might look to if you wanted to consider utilizing technology as a product? In this chapter, I am going to focus on the following areas:

1 Software and apps
2 Information
3 'Things'
4 Services

Software and Apps
Clearly, if you are a software business then this will be your product by default. However, there are a number of businesses out there that have developed software to support their main business but who aren't in the business of software. For

those businesses there are sometimes opportunities to package up and sell that software, to competitors or other firms in the market. For example, in the 1980s the financial asset management giant Blackrock developed an internal platform called Aladdin (asset liability debt and derivative investment network). It started out as a system for bond portfolios but soon developed to become an enormous database and system covering risk analytics, portfolio management, trading, operations and accounting. Blackrock have subsequently licensed this to many of the world's leading asset management firms and investment banks. Whilst you may not have the same market opportunity in your industry, the point is if you have developed proprietary software it is a route to additional revenue – albeit that if you aren't a technology firm and didn't build in-house, you would need to think carefully before doing this and about how you would support and maintain such a system.

Another route to similar revenue streams is available through apps. Apps are clearly a subset of the wider category of software but are called out distinctly as they have developed a very specific and large market for which the term 'software' perhaps doesn't do justice. Unlike software, apps have a typically different revenue model with somewhere between 80 and 90 per cent of apps on the Google or iOS stores free to download. The value opportunity comes either through the extension of a paid product, data and advertising, or through in-app purchases. Apps do offer great potential to businesses as they are relatively inexpensive to develop (dependent on your ambitions, of course) and offer a huge market to go after. If sold as a product in their own right they are usually providing comprehensive functionality – either as a game or for productivity purposes (e.g. specific packages like art, media applications etc.). They can, however, also be used to enhance your existing products and drive additional revenue that way.

For example, take NEST, Google's smart thermostat. Thermostats are not typically expensive things to buy; however, the NEST thermostat is, relative to other thermostats, expensive. In part that is owing to its clever learning technology, but it is also in part thanks to its convenience, which is driven by the app. As an owner I can say with certainty it's incredibly useful when you've been away on holiday for a week to be able to switch your heating off for the week and then remotely, on the morning you travel back home, use the app to turn your heating on. There are plenty of people, like me, who are willing to pay a bit more than they need to in order to benefit from this convenience. This is an example of an app that is there to enhance the product and thus support a higher retail price than it might otherwise achieve.

An example of data or advertising exists commonly in things like reward apps – for example, most popular coffee or food stores now have an app that allows you to sign up and collect reward points. Those apps can provide your business with a rich source of data – more information about your clients than you would otherwise be able to collect and the opportunity to target promotions to them, perhaps, for example, based on their location. Apps can also work well to enhance physical experiences – many zoos, holiday parks and theme parks utilize apps to provide on-site navigation, promotions, data capture and also geo-information to improve the experience. I once worked with a developer who had built an app for a zoo. They installed simple Bluetooth beacons around the zoo that interacted with the app on a guest's phone. As guests walked up to enclosures the app would receive the signal from the beacon and present the individual with information on the animal, videos and other content. In a very nice touch, clearly thinking about the 'experience' and recognizing that mobile phones tend to make people pretty antisocial, the developers focused on building a quiz for each animal enclosure – that way encouraging families and friends to interact with the app together as a team to solve the quiz, rather than playing with their phones on their own.

Differentiation is a key opportunity with apps as an enhancement or 'add on' to traditional products and whether you are a personal trainer looking to provide your clients with a unique app to track their progress and fitness level, or a zoo trying to bring their exhibits to life, there is opportunity here.

Information

There are a number of opportunities to build products or product enhancements based around information. If you are a data-rich business and collect information that others in your market would struggle to collect themselves, then you have an asset you may be able to monetize in the form of a data or business intelligence product. For example, let's say you run a large business installing boilers across the UK. Your customers are typically housing developers and for that reason they will specify the brands and models to be used and you will supply and fit. Let's say you also have a team of individuals who service boilers – either those you have fitted or others you have taken on after installation. Over time, you will naturally have the opportunity to build up insight and data on the market that could be useful to two of your stakeholders – the manufacturers of the boilers themselves and the housing developers. For example, you may be able to provide the manufacturers with information on their share of the new-build market, i.e. you will know how many of a certain brand you install each year versus the total installations you undertook. In the case of house-builders, you will build up some interesting insight into the boiler manufacturer's performance over time through your servicing activities – which are most reliable etc. That may also be useful for the manufacturers themselves! You could package either of these information sources up as a subscription service – for this you would need a database and a business intelligence tool on the front end to provide the reporting capability and perhaps charge an annual subscription to access the data (see Chapter 5.2).

Other opportunities include providing access to proprietary content. For example, monetizing content you are an expert on – written content such as insight, how-to guides, articles or media (music, video, photos etc.) can generate revenue. Newspapers do this well and have had to take their physical products and move them online in order to remain competitive, with many adding a subscription charge to access them and additional licence fees to other online businesses that want to reproduce any of the articles.

Online courses are another area growing in popularity and as a market in its own right. If you have expertise in a particular area, you could consider monetizing this either directly (pay to train) or as a product enhancement to improve the overall value proposition of your main product.

Physical Goods and the Internet of Things

If you are a business that manufacturers physical products (i.e. tangible things rather than say services, content or digital goods), there are opportunities to consider how technology can further enhance these to make them more attractive. I've already provided the example of the thermostat; consider another example in recent times – the humble doorbell. A basic doorbell should cost you no more than £20 at a local hardware store, but firms like Amazon who have built more advanced technology into them are charging 5–10 times that amount. Doorbells that show you a video of who is at the door and connect again to your phone (via an app) provide useful functionality that people will pay extra for.

The Internet of things (IoT) is a huge market and growing – and will continue to grow as people demand more sophistication from everyday items. To the extent you are making physical products or everyday items, you should consider the extent to which you can enhance with technology and command a premium price for your product. It also offers interesting revenue model opportunities. Take printers as an example. Printer manufacturers traditionally made money selling hardware and cartridges – i.e. they were trading businesses that had to sell more product every day in order to generate income. Many printers now come with 'intelligent' ink cartridges and connect themselves to the Internet so that you purchase a monthly subscription for ink rather than paying as and when required. Suddenly, printer businesses have been able to generate nice, predictable subscription income from what once was a lumpier business through the adoption of more sophisticated technology into the equipment.

Services

Services are another popular area for the use of technology as a product. Customer service-type offerings are not revenue generators in their own right but can greatly enhance an experience or product. Take online banking – you don't pay for it but its value to you, I suspect, will be enormous and without it the main product (i.e. your bank account) would be materially less attractive. Similarly, many firms offer client portals or customer portals as opportunities to generate differentiation for the main product – not just in financial services (though of course there are many examples there). It's not just customer service for which you can utilize technology to support; other forms of professional services are increasingly digitizing too. For example, architects, designers and similar are now offering services on a digital model – engaging with clients exclusively, reducing overheads and providing a new engagement model. The fundamental product is still the same (in the case of an architect, they ultimately need to produce a set of drawings), but the mechanism for engaging with the client and the supporting product service can be digitized. In the same way, there are plenty of examples of firms adopting things like VR and AR (augmented reality) in order to bring things such as buildings or other physical assets in digital form to life to greatly enhance the client experience.

The application of video technology to the mass mobile market has also created new forms of service technology – I've seen golf coaches in Spain coaching players on a golf range in the UK via a mobile app on video call; doctors, music tutors and other more traditional services are being delivered digitally on an increasing scale. I'm not saying it will replace the traditional methods entirely – but these are all areas you can look to if you are seeking to add a digital product to your service-based business.

4.4.2 STRATEGIES FOR TAKING THINGS FURTHER
Identify What's Possible
Identifying what is possible is your first step – you need to be honest with yourself and work out which, if any, of these opportunities are possible within your business. Asking yourself some of the questions below will help:

1 How will this fit in with your existing customer journey or product offering? Will it make sense to customers for you to offer this?
2 Do people need this product? Is there a market for it?
3 If so, how big is that market? Is it worth your time/what can you afford to invest and still make a return?
4 What is the route to reaching that market and is that a channel you have access to/could get access to?
5 Do you have the assets required to create this product? If not are you able to acquire them or develop them? (See the section in a moment on data quality for more on this if you are thinking about a data-based product.)
6 Will you have the capability to support and maintain this product economically once you have launched it?

Identify Where Your Value Will Come From
One of the first things you will need to identify is where your value will come from. The first section in this chapter will, I hope, have given you some ideas as to how you might develop

a technology revenue stream, and you may have other ideas beyond those I have suggested (after all, I certainly won't claim that the previous section is the definitive work on the subject!). However, what you really need to do is work out where your revenue will come from – you've essentially got three options:

1 Revenue that will come directly from the product – i.e. you will sell the software, data service, app or whatever it is you have decided to develop, either on a subscription basis or pay as you go/price per unit basis;

2 Revenue that will come from one of your other products that your technology product has made more valuable/ interesting/distinct from competitors – which means you can charge a premium price. This is an important point to think hard on – don't just assume that because your product contains a technology aspect, it can be monet- ized. There are such things as 'superfluous strengths'; i.e. things you are good at but that are kind of irrelevant for the market you are targeting. Don't allow your time and effort to be wasted on these;

3 Revenue that will come from third parties such as advert- ising and your technology product is a way to generate the advertising revenue.

Working out which of the above apply is going to be impor- tant since your focus when developing the product will change depending on the revenue stream. As a case in point, if your revenue is coming from the product itself, then your focus needs to be on the problem your product is solving and the functionality required to do that, i.e. making sure you build a high-quality product that does indeed solve the problems your potential customers are facing in a way other products out there currently don't. However, if your revenue is going to come from advertising, for example, you need to understand how the firms you intend to generate advertising revenue from value data and what it is they are trying to achieve. Yes, the functionality of your product will still be important to allow you to attract people/companies to it, but you also need to consider the way in which the advertisers are going to want to utilize the product to target those customers. Take Facebook as an example. Of course they focus on user experience (and do this very well) to ensure that people all around the world want to use their product and post information about their lives on a daily basis. However, if they only focused on making it a great product for posting photos and sharing information with friends they might be at risk of ignoring their core revenue stream – advertising. That requires them to also think about not just the data they capture and the functionality they provide, but also the <u>way</u> in which they structure that data and aggregate it so they can then use that for the purposes of providing a better and more useful experience for advertising. There will undoubtedly be many design decisions they have taken in order to ensure the product remains relevant for advertisers that they may not have taken if their sole focus was just on making a great product for the general public.

Data Quality and Segmentation

If you are going to make an information-based product, and in particular data-focused rather than other forms of content (articles, media etc.), then it is essential to focus on data quality.

If you are comfortable with the quality of the data today, do you have monitoring or cleansing processes in place to maintain quality in the future? If you are providing a data product, then this is important to consider since folks are not going to pay (for long) to consume inaccurate information. You will also need to build segmentation into your data model in order to provide clients with data relevant to their needs in a way that doesn't require lots of coding or product development each time you encounter a new client with a slightly different requirement. If you are looking for suggestions on how to improve the quality of your data, I cover this in Chapter 5.2, which focuses on business intelligence.

Bring in Expertise

The point of this chapter is not to provide you with a start-to-finish guide of everything you need in order to build a technology product – that would be impossible. Rather, the point is to provide you with ideas to get you thinking about opportunities to develop a technology revenue stream and, if this is viable, the sorts of things you need to think about before you get going to ensure you get proper value from it. This means you will leave this chapter with ideas and a framework perhaps, but certainly not all the skills you need to execute it. Bring in expertise to help you with this – either full time into your business or through consultants, but either way don't attempt to build a product until you have the right people in post. You can certainly 'get by' without some of these things when you are building something for you to use and you alone, but if you are going to sell it and for this reason have people judging your brand and business on it, then you can't afford not to invest in the right resources. Fortunately, there are various things you can do to help the economics work more easily – remind yourself of the things we discussed in the valuation chapter (Chapter 2) to help determine the most appropriate manner to fund and account for development and resource required. Keep in mind the availability of things like R&D tax credits if they exist (as in the UK) as another way of making the economics a little more palatable.

Joint ventures with technology firms are also worth considering if you are new to this but are sure you have an asset that can be monetized digitally. Joint ventures will allow you to focus on those things you are good at, and bringing in a partner with complementary skills who can focus on the technical areas you are less familiar with can be a smart way to accelerate your concept-to-launch timetable.

Technical Infrastructure

Technical infrastructure is going to be an important decision whatever product you build. If you build software, you will need to decide whether to develop and host yourself (SaaS) or provide as a download (on premise). See the Cloud Topic (Chapter 5.4) for more information in this area.

If you are looking at offering a data service, then you need to ensure you have a data warehouse with database queries optimized to return data quickly and for multiple users to whatever front-end tool you decide to use (see Chapter 5.2 for more ideas here).

It's worth bearing in mind that the infrastructure required to support a single business, i.e. yours, will be very different from that required to support 1,000 businesses. Data security will need to be considered more carefully if hosting multiple clients' data on the same database; you need to ensure it is segregated from one another, for example.

Choose the Right Development Methodology

Choosing the right development or project-management methodology to oversee the development of your product is important and will in part be determined by the sort of product you are developing. Read about the different methodologies available to you in Chapter 6 in this book to help identify the most appropriate way of doing this.

As a personal preference I strongly favour the more agile and iterative development methodologies over the more traditional; this is a way of de-risking the development materially since you have earlier sight of the product and therefore more frequent opportunities to seek client feedback. In addition, thinking about your MVP (minimum viable product) and working out what it is you really need to build to test whether a market exists for your product is sensible and, naturally, highly compatible with an agile approach to developing the product.

Support

You will need to consider whether or not your existing customer service and support arrangement will be sufficient to support a new technology product. In part this will be driven by the size of the market. For instance, in the earlier examples of the boiler installer, the number of users might be relatively small in what is a niche B2B market; the price they pay per user, of course, may still be material. In contrast, an app focused on providing a retail experience could reach hundreds of thousands or millions of people. Consider how you can respond to queries and requests for help with that volume of usage on the app.

Likewise, if you are building 'things' and have decided there is an opportunity to make them more digitally intelligent (e.g. smart devices) you will need to consider your current installer and support base. Are they capable of installing or supporting more advanced technology? And if not, are you able to train them to do this? You don't want to end up having to double up on resource owing to a lack of up-front thought on the skill set required to support your technical advances.

4.4.3 CASE STUDY

BUSINESS MONETIZING DATA ASSET

A colleague of mine worked with a business that started out providing loss-management services to the aviation sector. Over time, and due to the nature of the work undertaken, the business had built up a large database of aircraft that was managed by a data division. The business sought external investment to help the business grow and at the point of investment was just about breaking even. This revenue largely came from services provided to airlines, whereby data in varying formats (much of it on paper) was sent into the business that then digitized it, organized and enhance it, and then presented it back to them in an easy-to-consume format on CD-ROM. This data included aeroplane maintenance history, flight logs, servicing and repairs information, financing information, and other information required by the insurance and financing industries.

Due to the fact that this was a very different business model to the main business, which was effectively a loss adjustor, it was decided to spin the business out as a separate entity and bring in another team experienced in technology and data services to develop and grow the business in its own right. The first investment in technology was to build an online web-based product to service data via the Internet to clients. A challenge faced was that the data that fed this server sat in disparate data sets across the business and to amalgamate and clean it into one database utilizing traditional methods would have taken three to four years. This timeframe is a typical private equity hold period and therefore too long to consider. The business invested in a search and indexing tool to sit over existing databases and act as a consolidation layer over existing data to address this issue. Since it required little reworking of existing databases, it took years off the project and as a result the web interface was developed and launched as a new product nine months later.

An issue raised by clients was the fact that previously they would have downloaded the data from CD to be used in internal analytics tools; this wasn't possible over the web at the time due to download speeds and sheer volume of data. Therefore, the business invested in a second technology product, customized APIs for their clients. This was sold as a separate revenue stream to the core subscription product and added value instantly as a result.

The business then decided to focus their attention on the financial services sector of the airline market since they were one of the more profitable business segments in a struggling market. The business recruited financial service professionals to work alongside their technology team and together they developed an online benchmarking tool that provided a risk score relating to the aircraft data useable by financial analysts. This meant for any given plane it was possible to view a risk score based on its maintenance history, accidents, flying time, type of aircraft, age etc. This was then sold into the financial services sector heavily in the years that followed 2008 to assist portfolio managers who were dealing with challenging marketing conditions. It helped focus teams on where the real risks lay for new deals and required the business to build up great trust with senior risk-management and lending committees to ensure the scoring metric was a credible indicator.

Each investment was aimed at generating revenue and increasing customer stickiness to provide a real market-leading service, whilst ever focused on driving an EBITDA growth that meant the business could be sold within a sensible hold period. Third parties were involved, to provide expertise relating to change governance, technical expertise, and product and market expertise.

Projects were governed formally with appropriate support from the top team down, structured disciplines ranging from Prince2 to Agile were utilized, and whilst budgets were set, they were flexed to ensure that the product quality wasn't hindered. This process was managed via the Board. The team believed that the project governance had a positive impact on the outcome and noted the need to change their approach to project governance as time progressed. The team noted, for example, that Prince2 worked very well for the initial project to move their CD-ROM project on to the web but subsequent projects needed to be constantly iterated and improved, and therefore Agile was a more appropriate methodology to deliver this. This shift in governance model was important to the projects' success, not only through the rigour that it applied to them but also through culture change it introduced into the businesses, moving the business from what was perceived as a risk-adverse slow-paced business to a high-paced one.

The investment in technology enabled a barely profitable division of a business to spin out on its own and within several years turn a profit of over £2m.

4.4.4 CHAPTER SUMMARY

- There are a number of reasons why you may consider developing a technology product – either as a result of your decision to utilize an asset you have or because a competitor or market is moving in a way that demands it.
- Typical types of technology products you can provide can be grouped into:
  - Software and apps
  - Information
  - Things
  - Services
- Identify the art of the possible up front and be realistic about the assets you have and those you lack before you get started.
- Identifying your revenue model and source of value will be important – will this product generate revenue in its own right or support other revenue streams?
- Data quality is essential for information-based products and is something many businesses struggle with.

- Infrastructure is a key consideration for many of these products – scaling the infrastructure is a different challenge when selling products externally than when scaling for internal use.
- Data security is another important consideration, since you will be responsible for protecting your client's data.
- The development and project-management methodology you choose is important (see Chapter 6 for more information).
- Finally, consider support carefully to ensure you don't overload your existing teams with the introduction of a new product and damage your other client relationships or products in the process.

Section 5

Technology for Profit Growth

Clearly, revenue growth as described in the prior sections has the ability to drive profit growth by virtue of the fact it is adding to the top line. However, it is also possible to grow profits, as we know, through cost savings, and the following chapters focus on those technologies that lend themselves better to cost savings.

Cost and efficiency savings are probably the most common objectives cited for businesses investing in technology. This is true across almost every industry. For example, in financial services this has meant integrating back-office systems and creating new process-management systems that are more automated. Consider the differences in things like loan applications, mortgage applications and even customer services enquiries now in contrast to say 10 years ago. At that point, much of those processes would have been done through engagement with staff; now much of this has been replaced by technology-driven systems.

Likewise in retail, self-service checkouts, online purchasing and brand mass marketing through social media have all allowed businesses to reduce headcount and gain efficiencies through investments in technology.

The manufacturing sector has always been a big investor in technology; however, perhaps now more than ever the gap between the resources that larger businesses have invested in automation, robotics and technology to enable process improvements versus that available to smaller businesses is greater than ever.

There are also some technology-related investments that are common across many industries that enable profit and efficiency improvements. For example, the use of business intelligence software (that is, data analytics and reporting software) in order to identify inefficiencies and opportunities for improvement is seen across many sectors. It's also an area in which many businesses, despite the availability of these software products, are still failing to utilize to their full potential.

The following chapters focus therefore on specific areas in which technology investments can deliver or enable cost and efficiency savings and thus an improvement in the profitability of the business.

5.1

Digitizing Process

5.1.1 OVERVIEW

Process-management software, generally referred to as BPM solutions (business process management), is a term used to describe technology that you can use to streamline, control and digitize processes. There is often also an automation component to the software. This part varies considerably depending on the sector, type and use case for the software and is a rapidly changing and developing area of technology. In fact, I am almost certain by the time this book goes to print (as I write I expect that to be November 2020) some of what I talk about here will be out of date or further developed than I articulate here.

This is a broad subject and I would suggest one of the most heavily invested areas within businesses from a technology perspective since the 1980s – i.e. businesses have repeatedly come up with the investment case that says, 'We currently operate our business in a certain way and believe that investment in newer process technology can help us do that thing more efficiently, at less cost and free up human time' etc.

Many businesses will be familiar with the problems that surround process management – consistency of or adherence to processes that exist, efficiency of processes, complexity of processes, or in lots of cases processes that don't exist at all!

One of the challenges around process control is that in most businesses, processes are often created out of necessity and therefore not always carefully designed. In order to put technology around such processes requires not just the technology, but also time to rework the process steps themselves. This is an important point and worth thinking about. When was the last time you sat down in your business and actually designed a process? I suspect it's more likely someone came to you and asked what they should do in a situation they hadn't encountered before. You probably gave it some thought for a few moments and then gave them a response and thus a new process was born (inadvertently), and likely to be followed every time that situation arises in the future (regardless of whether that was your intention or not).

There are examples of business process-management systems everywhere. Consider some of the examples below:

CUSTOMER FACING

Application forms – for example, filling in an online application for a mortgage or car insurance. Without a system, you would fill in a paper mortgage application form and hand it in or send it to a bank or building society. An employee of that bank would then input that information into their systems for processing. This in turn would then be printed and walked over to one of the credit lender desks who would assess your application and make a decision. After this, your file would be updated, walked or posted back to the customer admin team who would write or phone to inform you of the decision. BPM systems have clearly made that simpler and more automated – simply by structuring data-capture forms online, automatically routing documents to the next step and (one hopes!) providing the manager in charge of mortgage applications with better intelligence on where things are in the process to ensure nothing is missed or overlooked.

Likewise, customer service processes – we will have all experienced automated customer service systems that involve logging queries, having them automatically routed to the right department based upon the content of them, the responses logged, and alerts sent back to the original customer when a response has been submitted.

INTERNALLY WITHIN A BUSINESS

Within businesses there are many use cases for process management, the most common including things like expenses, sign-offs, holiday forms, employee on-boarding, budget requests, document approval, e.g. sales quotes etc.

It's important to distinguish between two different categories of process-management systems – there are process-management technologies that are designed to improve the work that humans undertake and then there are those that are designed to do the work humans currently undertake.

This isn't to say these things can't be used in combination, in fact that is the general trajectory and certainly in the short to medium term presents the biggest value opportunity to most businesses. However, it is important to recognize the difference between these things as you will need to decide whether you are trying to make your people more productive or trying to reduce the number you need (or both). It's also worth noting that I deliberately refer to 'AI-based systems' below as clearly the application for AI (artificial intelligence) is much wider than simply process improvements.

Process-management systems do vary but there are usually common elements to them (the slight exception to this being AI, primarily because AI-based systems, given the nature of them, are sometimes less 'off the shelf' and more bespoke for each use case).

Generally, most have the following components:

i.   Process designer – some form of visual design tool that allows you to draw out the process as it should be undertaken. In some cases, this is purely a visual aid; however, in most tools now this also serves as the business logic and workflow engine that your process will rely upon for knowledge of what information it needs to capture from who, and then what it needs to do with that information. Robotic Process Automation (RPA) tools tend to feature a step-by-step designer that allows you to visually stitch together the steps you need to take to complete a task – for example a 'logging in' process might require you to map out that the RPA tool needs to go to a specific web address, find the username box, enter the username, find the password box, enter the password, submit the data back to the server etc.;

ii. Form design/data capture – all process-management tools require a mechanism for capturing data for use later in the process. In the earlier example of a mortgage application this can be quite complex data; in other cases (document approval, for instance) it could be as simple as capturing a document as an attachment, what sort of document it is, and the workflow tool might then do the rest. For RPA tools this is slightly different and usually involves helping the tool locate the data required – for example, in the case of invoice automation, showing the system which folder the invoices are stored in, showing it how to identify the next invoice in the queue and finding the number on the invoice itself that represents the amount to be input into a finance system;

iii. Business rules/decision engines – at the most basic level, process-management tools will need to know what sort of information must be completed before moving the process to the next stage, or which users are allowed to see/approve what information. At the more complex end of the spectrum, the business rules and decision engines are more powerful and can make decisions in place of people. As a case in point, there are numerous examples of automated decision-making in finance, such as decisions on loan approvals based on credit scores and information submitted on the application form. For RPA tools, error handling and rollback mechanisms are important too – if your robot goes horribly off-piste you need to be able to do something about it!

iv. Workflow/execution – process-management tools will generally have a component that is sitting on a computer or server running in the background orchestrating the processes. It is the component that recognizes someone has just filled in an expenses application and as such knows it needs to trigger the next sequence in the process and send that form to a line manager for approval etc. In the case of RPA it might be monitoring an inbox to see if a new invoice has come in and then triggering the robot to do something with it;

v. Reporting – most process-management platforms provide the capability to report on your processes. This can be useful with high volume/low value processes, to see where you are losing time on a regular basis, and likewise for low volume/high value processes where the process inefficiencies may not be repeated on a regular basis but have a material impact on the business when they do (perhaps taking time away from high-earning or fee-earning staff).

The above is a general and conceptual way of looking at these systems. As noted earlier, there are different types of business process-management tools, aimed at businesses of varying sizes and focusing on specific uses cases. Some of the most common variations on process-management systems are listed below:

Improving Work That Humans Undertake

i. Large BPM/case management systems. These are generally platforms that are heavily customizable, often for complicated business processes that may involve integrations with other systems and services and which have a greater requirement for complicated business rules.

The sort of use case that falls into this category would be our mortgage application example (see pages 114–15). Almost certainly, such an application will need to integrate into banking systems, send data to and from credit reference agencies, do something with the response from a credit reference agency (i.e. interpret the rating versus the bank's own rules and procedures) whilst ensuring all data is encrypted at all times (during transport and whilst 'at rest'). Generally, these take longer to implement, require more traditional 'coding' and technical support and are aimed at bigger businesses or businesses for whom scale would be impossible to achieve without the relevant automated processing benefits such a system can provide. Typically, an investment in such a system would be made if fundamental to a business's competitiveness or competitive advantage. For example, a retail bank would struggle to compete today without an online mortgage application process hence it is a required investment. However, the firm probably won't invest the same time and effort in their holiday request application, which isn't required for their competitive advantage. Implementation time is in the months to years category.

ii. Smaller mid-level systems, often referred to as 'low code' business process automation systems. Generally, these are more 'drag and drop'-based systems and referred to as 'low code' as they claim to require little programming. In reality, that is not quite the case; most will require at least some basic grasp of formulas and Excel-style programming and others considerably more. However, they are generally the sort of thing a technically competent end user could implement rather than requiring a programmer or IT professional.

These systems tend to be cloud-based (but not always) and rather than requiring the sort of customization and investment the larger systems require, often operate on a professional services + per user per month-type pricing model. These systems are great for internal processes or simple external processes for which integration with other systems is not a big consideration, the processes are reasonably straightforward, and the process can be relatively well contained within the single system. Implementation time for these systems can be as little as a few days or weeks and many now include 'starter apps', which are common business process applications that you simply need to 'tweak' to fit your own processes. Again, in practice this might require a little more than advertised, but is generally much quicker to implement than the bigger systems.

Doing the Work That Humans Undertake

i. Robotic process automation. As mentioned in the intro-
    duction, the two types of systems mentioned above
    generally make the assumption that people will be
    involved in the process and the technology and automa-
    tion (workflow and decisions) are going to make it easier
    for them to do their job. Robotic process automation
    attempts to take people out of the process and therefore
    it is entirely about the automation. Clearly, the more you
    automate, the surer of your process and data quality you
    need to be, and that shouldn't be overlooked when consid-
    ering RPA. Typically, this works best where there are very
    repetitive tasks that follow strict rules and procedures.
    For example, if you have a process whereby multiple

people from the accounts team are taking invoices from an invoice inbox, saving the attachments down, opening the finance system and keying in the invoice data, and you can be pretty sure on the uniformity of the invoice from a particular supplier from one month to the next, then that might be an obvious candidate for RPA. Worth noting – you can't take people out completely. You will always need a contingent who are overseeing and monitoring the processes and who can step in when things go wrong (a bit like those folks in supermarkets who oversee the self-service checkouts).

ii. Artificial intelligence-based systems. These systems are the most complicated and have the greatest potential, but at the moment they are also the most embryonic relative to their long-term potential. It's a very broad subject and there are many subcomponents to it, some of which you may be familiar with – such as machine learning and natural langue processing (NLP). These systems use a variety of technology components and algorithms in an attempt to develop truly independent intelligent systems. In time, the potential for AI is enormous, but right now its application to most businesses is limited to specific use cases. The situation with AI at the moment is that it requires significant financial investment, data, time and expertise to develop a proprietary system, resources only the biggest companies possess. However, owing to its iterative and embryonic nature, it also requires an entrepreneurial and nimble culture, a trust that the investment will yield a future return but which at present is impossible to quantify, as well as a lack of technology 'baggage' (rubbish data and old systems). These latter qualities are generally characteristics of smaller companies, that is to say, small businesses are far more likely to have the culture and mindset that would make an AI project successful, whilst only bigger companies have the funds and can afford the necessary expertise. A dilemma indeed!

5.1.2 HOW TO GET THE MOST OUT OF PROCESS-MANAGEMENT SOFTWARE

Understand How these Tools Could Positively Impact Your Value Chain

Typically, business process management targets a reduction in cost and an improvement in efficiency. Therefore, it can have a material impact on the operating profit margin when used effectively. The extent to which it can do this and the processes on which you choose to implement it will vary based on your business. However, these systems tend to be of biggest benefit where one or more of the following are true:

i. Processes are well defined (or can be) and there is a need to ensure process consistency, i.e. you want to make sure every time someone produces a sales quote it is signed off by the finance director, head of sales and operations director before it is released to the client, and you don't want this process to run based on the diligence of sales people remembering to follow a process;

ii. Existing ways of working are inefficient, involve lots of manual processing, moving data around over email, manual rekeying between systems;

iii. Processes for which people spend a lot of time in the business asking, 'Where are we with this?', 'Who is dealing with that?'

iv. Lots of people doing the same thing (an opportunity for RPA) or lots of people making the same decisions (AI-based tools). For example, processing invoices (RPA as a possible solution) or teams of people making credit decisions by interpreting information from a standard loan application form (AI opportunity);

v. Declining profit margins (% not £) or disproportionate increases in administrative staff costs. In earlier stage rapidly growing businesses, IT often has to play catch-up during the growth stage (no one starts a business by designing their IT architecture!). This is particularly true as growing businesses typically undergo a series of pretty transformational operating model changes as they go from 1 person to 10 people to 50 people to 100 people etc. You will often see these businesses becoming increasingly inefficient at the start of each 'growth phase', with people often doing things manually in order to deal with them quickly rather than fixing the root cause of problems. Therefore, in cases where there are declining profit margins or disproportionate staff cost increases in administrative roles, this may indicate an opportunity for BPM value add.

You will need to identify whether your opportunity lies in helping your people work more efficiently or replacing them with machines. As a case in point, if you are running a business providing executive coaching then you probably want to use these tools to ensure your coaches spend as much time coaching as possible and as little time on admin. In other words, the value opportunity is to improve the processes your staff undertake rather than replacing them. You might decide to implement a process-management tool that makes booking appointments, tracking notes and follow-ups as simple as possible. You could of course also implement an RPA tool alongside it to do the repetitive, boring jobs like processing invoices.

By comparison, if you worked in a business that specialized in data entry, you might decide investing more money in RPA tools to replace some of the staff you have is a more appropriate form of process improvement. However, you would then need to ensure you automated enough of the process to allow you to reduce headcount – by that I mean you would be better off automating everything that just one individual does and saving the cost of one individual than automating a small part of a task that everybody does. If you do the latter, you still need everyone in the business to do the rest of their job; you've essentially then just invested time and money in making their lives a bit easier by taking away part of their job!

Be clear from the outset what you want to achieve and how you can measure success (fewer people in the business, same number of people but more revenue, time savings for particular groups of staff etc.). It doesn't have to be a financial metric you measure, but if you choose to measure something else like time saving, just be clear (in your own mind at least) that it will indeed lead to financial improvements overall.

Choose Your Processes with Care
It makes sense to start with processes that are smaller and self-contained and build out from there. If this is your first move

into BPM then you should try and identify a process that will have a measurable impact or visible change at the end. For example, it's going to be pretty obvious in the mortgage business if suddenly all applications no longer involve a human (i.e. an office with a bank of empty desks is a clear sign the system is doing its job). However, you could equally start with just one element – such as digitizing the application forms – and perhaps measure the increase in applications post-implementation or the reduction in application-processing staff as evidence it is adding value as intended.

You should also think about process design before simply attempting to replicate an existing process in digital form. As I mentioned earlier, most business processes (particularly in smaller companies) aren't designed – they typically just evolve out of necessity. Therefore, step back and consider whether there are better, more logical ways to do something. This is particularly true if you decide to use either RPA or AI-based tools, as computers don't get bored doing lots of repetitive tasks. Processes involving humans typically factor in some level of complexity and job satisfaction and hence may not be optimized for pure efficiency – this doesn't need to be replicated if a robot is going to do the job instead.

Finally, it may seem obvious, but apply this care to those processes with the greatest value to your core business. Don't spend vast sums automating stuff that is peripheral to your main lines of business; automating the company's room-booking process or expenses process may sound like a good idea and the mark of a forward-thinking business, but unless it's really going to help you make a lot more money don't bother!

Prepare to Code (a bit)

There are a number of good off-the-shelf BPM systems (Kissflow, Nintex, Asana etc.). Whilst all offer a level of 'drag and drop' and will advertise that these systems require no coding knowledge, in practice if you want to do anything half decent you will need to utilize coding skills at some point. This certainly doesn't need to be a barrier to progress or put you off – it's a pretty common skill set now – but do go into it with your eyes open and the expectation that coding will be required. And if you don't have that skill set, learn it or buy it before you start on this journey. The same is going to be true for the more automated RPA systems and AI-based tools.

Limit Hand-offs Between Humans and Robots

More applicable to the RPA tools, these things work best when robots complete their processes and humans complete their own, separate, processes. Hand-offs between robots and humans generally reduce the efficiency opportunity you have, as the value you can get from a robot is the ability to complete lots of repetitive tasks quickly. Emphasis here is on the word 'complete'. You can only go as fast as the slowest point in the chain and if your robot can't complete a process without waiting for a human to intervene each time, you are reducing the potential efficiency improvements significantly and back to working at whatever pace your staff are capable of.

'Build It and They Will Come'

It can be hard to get buy-in for things that are truly transformational, particularly if you work with individuals with a limited capability for imagination. When trying to articulate why an investment in process-transformation technology would be worthwhile, it will be tempting to paint a picture of a future in which things are so different and automated that scepticism and cynicism sets in and it can be hard to convince people it is possible to achieve. As a result, you never get going. Sometimes it is simpler just to get on with it, following the advice in this chapter; start small, build something that creates demonstrable value and then others will see the benefit. You can then build out from there with a group of like-minded individuals until eventually you build enough that the capacity for process improvement and automation is in the hands of all staff rather than one or two experts. When people can start improving their own processes or automating tasks themselves, you will develop and progress much faster.

Consider RPA as a System Integration Tool
In older businesses one of the challenges when seeking to implement any form of digital transformation can be the limitations presented by older systems. It is not uncommon for businesses to have old systems that are fundamental to the core business and have many spreadsheets and downstream systems hanging off them but which don't do everything you want them to. You find businesses often want to replace these systems but can't because the work involved in unpicking all the dependencies and links to downstream systems is just too hard or risky. Take banks, for example, where in many cases some of the most fundamental systems in the bank's architecture powering cashpoints, payments systems and similar are the 'green screen' systems implemented in the 1990s. Here is where RPA has the potential to add real value and time savings

to a process – rather than spending years and man hours replicating all those dependencies in a new system, RPA can be used to rekey data from a newer system into an older one – thus ensuring downstream systems and dependencies are preserved in a cost-efficient manner.

Understand Limitations – Be Realistic
For the systems that are seeking to improve the processes humans undertake, be realistic about what you can expect people to do. Make sure whatever solution you implement is simple to use, intuitive and you build up gradually so people are comfortable using it. In the same way, introduce flexibility where you can – you don't want to end up introducing a 'the computer says no' culture.

For RPA systems, you are going to be reliant on a robot and as such the powers of common sense and reasoning are going to be limited to whatever you can anticipate in advance and build into the system. This means you need to have decent data – if you don't have decent data to work from then you need to accept your ability to automate is going to be limited and much better you spend time fixing the data first. The saying 'garbage in garbage out' is often used to describe rubbish data going into a system and then the MI out the back of it being meaningless. This concept is significantly more troublesome if you are no longer talking about simply MI being wrong but you have robots taking action off the back of it and those actions are incorrect!

RPA capability also needs to be recognized as still developing (i.e. limited). Whilst great leaps have been made so far in this area, you should remain aware that these systems are still very sensitive to the slightest change in an environment.

For example, I've implemented robotic process-automation systems to take data from spreadsheets and enter it into systems. However, as soon as a button on the screen moves or a field label or the values in a dropdown change there is every chance your robot will struggle, break and require human intervention to update its workflow.

As noted previously, AI-based tools have huge potential but you need to accept that they are costly and time-consuming to develop from scratch, require huge volumes of data to train, and hence my final suggestion in this section is going to be...

For AI-based Systems, Focus on Specific Use Cases Where Solutions Already Exist

There are a number of AI-based solutions for businesses out there that focus on specific use cases and subcomponents within AI. For example, there are now some very good systems that can read and interpret legal agreements using natural language processing technology. NLP is a subset of AI and is concerned with the reading and interpretation of human language – i.e. not just simply extracting the text from a document, but interpreting the text to extract facts and meaning from the language in the same way a human would. These systems have been trained to look at different types of legal agreements and then flag clauses that are either different from 'standard' clauses, those that require attention, or even suggest alternative wording. If you have a business that deals in large volumes of contracts and these contracts are fairly standard – e.g. perhaps you deal with a large volume of NDAs – then these tools can save time and money going to a lawyer each time and you can instead focus the legal expertise on dealing with exceptions or difficult points. Typically, these systems have been trained by lawyers to do 80 per cent of the work and then you get involved in the tailoring for your specific business and contracts. As a result, you shortcut much of the R&D required to arrive at a useful working product.

Virtual assistants or chatbots are other examples of off-the-shelf tools available that you can build upon to deliver some value relatively quickly, assuming of course that these tools are a good fit with your business model. Much of the hard work in inferring meaning and interpreting requirements from a user's input has been done for you; the implementation is about how you then choose to anticipate and answer the questions that will be specific to your business.

Machine learning is another subset within AI, focused on developing systems that are able to improve their capability and intelligence automatically. A good example of this is recommender systems – take, for example, online retail sites that look at a user's searches, past behaviour and purchases in order to recommend other relevant products. The more information the algorithm learns about the individual, the more accurate (in theory) its recommended products can be. There is an important point here worth noting: machine learning systems don't become more intelligent in isolation – they still require input, usually from humans, in terms of additional data points. In this example, the more data points the algorithm has on a particular individual's shopping and browsing habits, the more accurate it can be.

There are a number of firms out there who are developing machine learning and AI tools that are being modularized and as such offer smaller firms an opportunity to leverage the power and capability of AI but without quite the same investment in time and expertise up front. If you are considering the potential of AI and machine learning in your business, consider partnering with such a firm as a way to get you going. It will still be expensive, but much cheaper than doing it on your own.

5.1.3 CASE STUDY

A PROFESSIONAL SERVICES BUSINESS SEEKING TO IMPROVE EFFICIENCY

Many years ago, I worked with a professional services firm who worked on a fee-earning revenue model; that is, they employed highly skilled specialists who could be charged out to clients based on an hourly fee rate. The more hours they could bill, the more revenue they could make. Based on their existing operating model the only way they could increase revenues was to take on more fee-earning staff. Following some detailed process analysis work, the business identified that the fee earners were only able to dedicate around 60 per cent of their time to fee-earning work, with the rest spent on admin. This admin part of their job included working across multiple management systems, spreadsheets, and manually creating letters and forms when required. It was identified that implementing a new process-management system that reduced duplicate data entry and was capable of automating more of the documentation could allow the fee earners to increase the percentage of time they could dedicate to fee-earning work from 60 per cent to nearer 75. This represented a 25 per cent improvement opportunity and therefore could materially impact the business. The implementation focused on rolling out the new system to one team at a time, which meant results could be seen more quickly than if they tried to roll it out to the entire business in stages.

Some of the challenges the business faced, not unexpectedly, were cultural challenges (not everyone likes change) and technological challenges – many processes had more nuances than first anticipated and it's only when you attempt to code a process into a series of black and white stages and decisions that these become clearer. However, ultimately the business did succeed in the implementation and whilst the end results were not quite as high as they had anticipated, the business still saw an improvement.

5.1.4 CHAPTER SUMMARY

- Business process management (BPM) software aims to digitize and implement workflow around processes, often with an element of automation too.
- These tools can be applied to customer-facing processes, internally facing processes or processes that cover both.
- There are two main categories of systems: those that aim to make human work more efficient and easier to do, and those that seek to replace the work a human would do.
- Typical components of BPM software are process design, form/screen design, business rules, workflow, reporting.
- Systems can be large, complex implementations, but in many cases, in particular within small businesses, low code/no code systems are available.

- Robotic process automation and artificial intelligence have a big role to play here and this will become an increasingly large opportunity.
- You need to be clear on the impact these tools could have on your value chain and pick your processes carefully.
- Accept you will need technical expertise even for systems that profess to be no code/low code.
- Try and limit hand-offs between robots and humans where you can.
- Owing to the emerging nature of AI and machine learning and the cost of developing something proprietary in these areas, instead look for specific point solutions that have been developed with your particular problem in mind.

5.2

Business Intelligence

5.2.1 WHAT IS IT?

Business intelligence, or 'BI' tools, are software tools that allow you to take the outputs from different data sets within your business and combine them together to create interactive reports, dashboards, and ultimately generate insights that you can use to better understand your business and take action as a result.

These tools are visually rich, interactive and designed to allow a non-technical user to create dashboards and reports and then interrogate them – slicing and dicing the data in a more freeform and intuitive manner than traditional fixed reports.

Given the nature of the insight they provide, you could argue these tools are capable of supporting revenue growth, profit enhancement or cash generation. I've categorized them in the profit-enhancing category simply because whichever of the above you end up using them for, they save you a lot of time, effort and energy to get to that point and hence an expected improvement on profitability.

It's worth stating that I am focusing this chapter on those tools that are off the shelf and therefore easier to implement yourself, and if you don't have this capability already then this is definitely the place to start. However, it is worth noting there are some incredible data science businesses out there that have invested time and resources in building bespoke proprietary analytics engines that combine AI, algorithms and large data sources to offer analysis and predictive analytics on another level. These sorts of platforms can be very value adding and I've included a case study at the end to demonstrate the point. However, in the interests of focusing on some practical things you can do yourself in this area, most of this chapter will focus on the sorts of tools you can implement within your own business rather than services you can procure from data science firms.

To understand the power of these tools and how they differ from traditional reporting tools, we'll consider an example.

Let's say you run a national retailer with 20 stores in different parts of the UK selling your own brand of clothes. We will assume for now you have an EPOS system (electronic point of sale – i.e. a till capable of providing data in a format a computer could interrogate), a membership system that holds information on your club card members, a warehouse system that keeps track of stock levels, a finance system, an HR/payroll system keeping records on payments to staff and employee data, and then a finance system for posting the income and expenditure transactions to, for financial reporting.

Traditional software reports would probably exist in all of these systems separately. For example, you could perhaps generate a report from your till system showing you all the purchases this year – it would probably show the codes for the items purchased, the salesperson code, the dates purchased, price paid, whether the transaction was cash or card, a store code and a club card number where relevant.

The membership system might allow you to run a report of all your members showing names, ages, addresses, how long they have been a member etc.

Your HR system might produce a report showing you names and personal details for all employees, perhaps something on their qualifications, their position in the business and history of promotions and roles, length of service, training records, any disciplinary issues etc.

Your finance system would show you income and expenditure by month, by store and by P&L line item.

As you can see from the above, in isolation these reports are relatively useful but not really giving you much value above and beyond repeating back to you whatever data has been input. You may get some insight but I suspect not much. For example, your HR system could tell you the percentage of staff with a degree, but so what? Surely you need to know if that matters or not?

These traditional forms of reporting are generally pretty fixed in their format and require IT-skilled individuals to programme new variants on them if that is required.

The next level of sophistication would be to put all that data into a database and start to link it together. You could then say to your IT team, 'I would like to see a report showing me each store manager and for each of them I want to see their last 12 months' worth of revenue and profit figures.' IT would then build that report for you; you could run it and then analyse the results. Suppose you then saw that the Essex store was performing particularly well and the Canterbury store performing badly. You might hypothesize that the store manager's qualifications or length of service have something to do with this, so you ask the IT team to build another report showing you qualifications and length of service by individual. You wait for this to be built and then run it to examine the two individuals. Suppose you then find no difference and decide there may be other variables at play. You can see how these scenarios may well lead to quite a lot of back and forth with IT teams in order to arrive at a report that gives you an answer that you think makes sense. The challenge with these fixed reports is that they typically require coding and design in order to produce them and once built you can filter a little within the parameters on the report but you must use the same fixed formats each time.

A BI tool takes this forward several leaps. You would use the BI tool to create some basic interactive reports perhaps showing staff information, store information, profit information and maybe presented in a combination of charts and tables. The important thing here is that this report would be interactive and linked together. As such, if you selected a profit range on the filter, £2m–£4m for example, the report would automatically readjust just to show you information on the stores, staff members, club card members and purchases related to stores that make £2m–£4m profit. If you then drilled down further to select a specific store, the report would once again redraw itself showing you only individuals, purchases and customers linked to that store. Going further you might identify one or two key repeat club card members contributing to big purchases. Having discovered that you might then want to start again and simply filter those club card members for a view across all the stores where they have made purchases etc.

The point here is that these tools are designed to allow you to continuously filter related data sets without having to pre-determine strict formats or filters up front. So long as you can link the data together, you can pretty much cut and analyse the data on any metric within the data set. This is very powerful and, what's more, creating these reports (once the infrastructure is up and running) can be done without any particular IT or systems coding knowledge. The visual aspects of these tools are also important – being able to visualize data on a map, for example, can be far more meaningful than seeing a list of data grouped by postcodes or cities.

BI tools typically describe the front-end reporting tools that you use to create the dashboards and reports, but in practice, the business intelligence 'setup' contains a number of components, as outlined below.

Raw Data Sources

Raw data sources are just that, the raw data set that contains information you would want to utilize in your reporting tool. These can be systems, databases, Excel spreadsheets, flat text files, PDFs and many other formats too. In our example above they would be the outputs from each of the individual systems. Some of these systems may feature software known as APIs (Application Programming Interfaces, meaning there is a ready-made mechanism that will allow the system to talk to other systems in order to send and receive data without having to be explicitly linked together) whilst the others may simply produce a good old-fashioned spreadsheet download.

Extract and Transformation Tool (ETL)

These tools are designed to interact with the raw data sources in order to work them into a structured format and allow them to be utilized by a BI tool. They generally take data, manipulate it and then send the output into a database or data warehouse.

For example, let's consider our chain of shops. The EPOS system might produce something along the lines of the below:

Date Time Stamp	Store_ Code	Item_Code	Price_ GBP	Membership_ Card_Number
01/03/2011 13:42:56	7001	10298272	£24.99	029837273927
01/03/2011 16:42:56	5236	18230282	£29.99	978576283923

The club card system might produce something like this:

Membership_ Card_Number	Title	First_Name	Last_Name	Member_Since
029837273927	MR	John	Smith	1st June 2009
978576283923	MRS	Elaine	Wood	24th April 2001

You might decide you want all dates in the same format to make filtering simpler and based upon dd/mm/yyyy (or mm/dd/yyyy) stripping out times. You may also decide that you need to have some sort of user-friendly reference for the store codes and so you could use the ETL tool to convert the codes into a single store code – for example, you could tell it to always convert item_code 1234 to 'Canterbury'. You might even have two different EPOS systems in use and want to use the ETL tool to get both their outputs to look the same, i.e. in the same format with the same column headings etc. The ETL tool would then extract the data, transform it into a common format as you determine it should do, and put the resulting transformed data into a database.

Database/Data Warehouse

I am going to presume that we all know what a database is by now, but it's probably worth pointing out that the sort of database you choose will need to be thought through and will be determined based upon your available expertise, budget, levels of sophistication required and how many people need to use it. For example, a reporting tool for one or two people with a small number of records might work fine in Microsoft Access. However, if you want to build something capable of holding vast stores of data to be used by many different people concurrently, you will need a more robust system such as Google Big Query, ORACLE, SQL Server, cloud computing power etc., and this requires a bit more technical knowledge and expertise to get it up and running. Database design is an art form in its own right and it's worth getting in proper expertise to do it properly. You will need to think about table design (for example, you generally only want to store a single piece of information once) and establish links between tables so that the relationships between data sets are clearly defined. In our example above we would have a 'sales' table and a 'members' table and would want to set a relationship between the 'membership_number' fields in each table so the database knows it could link member 1234 in the members table with any member records in the sales tables.

It is worth spending a bit of time on this stage and getting this design right. Setting appropriate indexes on the tables (things that help the database search more quickly for information) and intelligent design can be the difference between databases that take ages to return the information you want and those that work with lightning precision and speed. As with all chapters in this book, the purpose of this is not to turn you into a database designer (you have a business to run!) but to point out this is a key component to consider, the role it plays in the overall BI setup, and to give you specific areas to focus on when working with a specialist.

Front-end BI Reporting Tool (usually referred to as a BI tool)
The main focus of this chapter is these BI tools I described in my earlier example. Examples of tools include Qlik, Tableau and Microsoft Power BI. They are the front-end reporting environments that sit on top of your data and allow you to create dashboards, tables, charts and to analyse the data. You can see in the example below there are some featured KPIs, graphs, tables and other visual representations of data. Clicking on any item in the screen re-cuts the entire report. For example clicking on a date would change the data displayed for that time period. Likewise, you might add a table showing different hospitals and clicking on each hospital would then re-cut the report to just show the data for that location. This is reliant on the tool being able to link the data together (more on that shortly) and of course the more you can do in your ETL and database tools in that regard, the less messing around an end user has to do in the BI tool.

Here is an example of a Qlik dashboard:

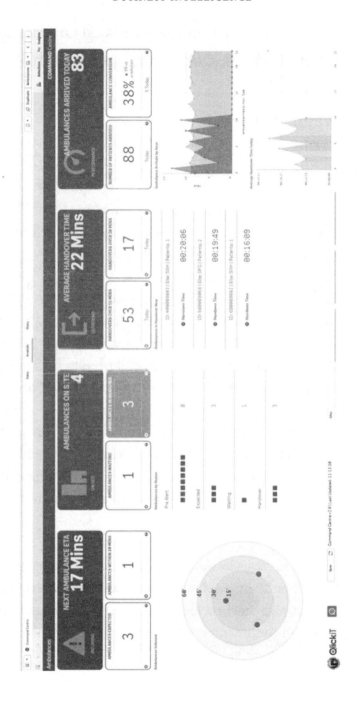

A number of these tools also have statistical functions built into them to allow you to do processes like forecasting and predictive analysis.

5.2.2 GETTING THE MOST OUT OF BI TOOLS

Understand the Questions you Need to Ask – What Are Your Value Levers and the Supporting Data Items That Will Add Context to Them?

This is perhaps an obvious but important first step. The BI tools I have described are very flexible and intuitive to use, and some of them also have the capability to analyse your data and suggest charts and insights that may be helpful for you. However, no BI tool is going to understand your business or market in the way that you do and it is highly unlikely insights and charts suggested by a tool are going to cover all the bases you require. In other words, you will still need to instigate the questions and perform the interrogation yourself in order to arrive at your own well-reasoned conclusion. The tool is just giving you a head start and rapid access to the data you need in order to do that. As a result, it stands to reason you need to be pretty clear on what your value levers are and the supporting data items. Let's revisit our retailer example, you might decide that:

- Revenue is driven by the products sold and the price they are sold for. The sales of products are driven by individual stores, which in turn are managed by staff members, located in specific geographies and that have customers who spend their money in them;

- Profit is driven by the revenues (above) less overheads. Overheads are driven by stores, which are managed by employees, and have outgoings that will vary based on geography and that will also have differing levels of customer returns.

Therefore, you might conclude you need information on sales by product, store and at product (item) level. You will also need employee data, customer (club card member) data, returns data and overheads data by store (invoices/entries in the finance system). You might also determine that to add more context to the analysis, date information would be helpful so that you can compare things over time. Budget data might also be useful in order that you can compare actuals with expectations. If you are looking for wider context, you might decide you will want to combine your own data with the dates and nature of notable public events (perhaps a list of public events, society weddings etc.) or even weather information (temperature per day, for example).

The purpose of walking though the above is to show that when you ultimately glean insight from your data set, you need to be able to work out how those insights relate back to changes or decisions you should be making in your business. Thus, starting with your value levers and extrapolating out is the simplest way of ensuring that what you come up with does in fact tie back to a driver of value in the business. For example, you might ultimately find on sunnier days you sell more shorts and T-shirts (makes sense) and so you could use that insight in future years to ensure you 1) have a process to monitor weather, and that 2) you are properly stocked with extra shorts and T-shirts ahead of weeks that are forecast to be hot.

Likewise, you might discover variances in product popularity by postcode, which may mean you change the product mix in each store to suit the expected clientele and thus reduce your working capital requirement.

Whilst the tool will allow you to combine and then slice and dice this data, it can't create data that isn't there. That is to say, if you know you need to look at things over time, you are going to need to ensure date information is in there. If you know you need to look at things by store, you need to ensure information on stores is in the data set. You can't simply point these tools at every field in every system you have and say 'get on with it'! You need to plan and think through the specifics of the data needed – once you have done that, then the reporting and analysis you do is going to be much simpler and quicker than it would be with more traditional methods and won't require much in the way of specialist IT input (once it's up and running).

Data Quality and Matching

Again, at the risk of pointing out the obvious, data quality is an absolutely critical part of this. You can't start with poor data and expect a BI tool to somehow magically unpick and do something with it. Rubbish in, rubbish out.

Now, it's important to distinguish between poor data and data that is in a poor format. The former is information that is either wrong, likely to be wrong or you have simply no confidence in its accuracy, i.e. the information is available, you just don't know if you can trust it. This is a fundamental issue and if that is where you are then you should halt any work on BI tools until you fix this. In the interests of helping you solve this problem I've listed a few suggestions below for tackling bad data, but it can be a big job to fix. Data in a poor format represents information you can trust, but the format or presentation of it is poor and without further work, is technically unusable. This might be so in the case of old systems where the outputs are typically pretty inflexible and it just needs reworking (ETL tools are good for this) or it might be where you have key 'linking' data in text form rather than IDs – for example, a need to match data between systems using something like a name and so you have to get some consistency into spellings. Again ETL tools can help with this; you can, for example, code them to replace all instances of 'ltd' 'limited' '.Ltd' with 'Limited' and so on, in order to increase the chances of matching. It can be time-consuming to do, and there are data scrubbing tools that can help, but it is well worth spending time on.

Strategies For Fixing Untrustworthy Data

If this is something you need to overcome, here are a few ideas that may help. There is often no silver bullet to these things and it does need patience and focus to get results, but without resolving this it's pretty hard to do anything useful.

Make data quality essential to process

This first one is the surest way to really fix poor data but often requires process rework. Data quality is often not driven by the diligence of the individual entering the data, but more by the extent to which bad data will prevent the inputter getting what they want! I will give you an example. I am sure you have an email account and let's say that you also have an Apple Music and Amazon shopping account. If I were to ask whether your name and address are correct on your Amazon account, you would be confident in confirming that it is indeed correct. Why? Because if it wasn't your purchases wouldn't reach you! Therefore you have to make sure your address is right in order to get what you want. Now consider your email account. It may be with Hotmail or Yahoo or Gmail but whichever it is, it's very likely that your home address information in that system is not up to date or correct. Why would this be the case, when the inputter is the same diligent individual who got it right on the Amazon database? The reason it won't be up to date is because you don't need it to be accurate in order to get what you want – in this example, to send an email. I am pretty sure that if every time you sent an email a copy of it was posted to the address on file you would soon make sure it was correct! The purpose of this is to show that the only way you can really ensure good data is to tie it to processes that can't function without it. If you have bad data coming from a system, consider what process changes you might be able to make in order to incentivize the inputter to get it right. For example, if you found in your HR system that the qualifications data for staff wasn't being kept up to date because it depended upon staff members updating it themselves, you might change the process for receiving any associated pay rise so that no pay rises are processed until qualification records are updated.

Fix historic data

Fixing the process is great for ensuring good data going forward, but what about all that old data you have? How you fix this often depends on the complexity of the systems involved and volumes of data. In cases where volumes are low, it's often easiest (although painful to watch) to employ an army of lower-paid individuals to manually go through and fix bad data than it is to spend the same time and cost setting up a clever automated tool for fixing the data.

In situations where the volumes are just too great, there are data-cleansing and scrubbing tools out there that will help clean up the data. However, those tools can't really change figures or facts without some other reference data to work from.

For very repetitive tasks where data can be referenced elsewhere, you could consider a simple RPA tool (see Chapter 5.1) to look up the right data in the reference source and update it in the system. In other words, this is a technology version of hiring an army of low-paid individuals to fix it manually.

Do as much messing around with the data outside the BI tool
Remember the point of BI tools is that they are designed to slice, dice and interrogate the data to provide insights you can action. They should be simple to use and allow non-technical users to create reports and generate insight. As soon as you introduce a need to manipulate or work on the underlying data itself, you make it much more complicated and it becomes about fixing or working with data on a technical level rather than getting any sort of insight from it.

Therefore, you should do as much of the transformation and linking work in the ETL tool or database itself. These tools can then be set up by technical individuals and ideally once set up, left alone to run on a scheduled basis, meaning all the BI tool user needs to do is create good-looking reports and utilize insight from the data.

Start Small and Build

As with some of the other technologies discussed in this book, starting small and building out from there is a good way to start. For this to work you still need to go through the process of identifying your value levers – but perhaps focus on one specific one. Let's say in our retail example we decide our biggest problem is decreasing revenues. We might therefore focus all our attention on understanding that particular problem and building a tool aimed at interrogating the components of revenue, and not worry about overheads and profitability for the time being.

Proof of concepts are great ways to get going and the good thing about these tools is that they are very easy to start and work with. Many are cloud-based and Power BI, for example, is included with certain Microsoft Office 365 subscriptions (so you may even find you have access to a version of it for no extra cost). I've done proof of concepts for firms start to finish in less than 72 hours and driven real value and actionable insight from them as a result. Yes, when you come to implement them in a production capacity it takes more work, but that is more about the setup of the infrastructure and other components (databases, transformations etc.) than it is about setting up the reports in the BI tool.

Picking a good partner is very useful and worth doing from the outset. Yes, you can build reports yourself, but if you want to save wasting a lot of time trying to understand how to structure databases or manipulate data with ETL tools, then work with a partner who can get you going more quickly.

Understand the Different Tools and Their Strengths and Weaknesses
I have no particular affiliation with any BI tool but it is worth knowing that each of the big tools out there have different strengths

and weaknesses. A quick Google search will present you with plenty of insight into the differences, so I am not going to repeat that here but more draw your attention to the fact that they are all different. For example, Qlik has a unique associative data engine and therefore performs more quickly than Tableau and Power BI. It's also very good at presenting data in tables whereas Tableau can be stronger in other areas of data visualization – maps, for example – and also has a more powerful forecasting/statistical component to it. That said, Qlik also has a GeoAnalytics capability and a forecasting/stats engine. If you are looking for a list of products to research I would suggest looking into the below:

- Qlik
- Tableau
- Power BI
- Thoughtspot
- Looker

Think Mobile

In practice, you will often be looking at these tools on a laptop or desktop PC. However, most of the major BI tools have a mobile offering and it's worth considering that element when you are designing your dashboards for users who work remotely. For example, if you have sales teams working remotely who are always on the go, providing them with a mobile-friendly dashboard they can quickly use to filter in on a subset of customer data for insight a few minutes ahead of a customer meeting might be more useful to them than a more comprehensive dashboard that requires them to find somewhere they can open a laptop and work from.

5.2.3 CASE STUDIES

A LEISURE BUSINESS

I worked with a business that operated a number of leisure sites around the UK. The business had a relatively old booking system and as a consequence reporting out of the back of it was limited. We worked with them to implement a simple ETL tool and BI tool over the top to help them gain access to their data. This was actually a very good use case for this tool in that it had many of the components that are required to create value, namely:

1 The business knew it had accurate data in their systems;
2 The business had a forward-thinking CEO who understood the potential of data to drive value in his business but didn't understand technically how to unlock it.

In other words, the barrier to progressing was a technical one rather than about cultural or data quality.

We decided to focus the proof of concept on a couple of things: the first was to help determine the impact of marketing to repeat customers versus general mailshots, and the second to better understand the make-up of the customer base by park.

The business had historically sent the same mailshot out to its entire database when running promotions. The hypothesis of the CEO was that more targeted and tailored comms to repeat customers was more likely to yield results than mass mailing but he wanted the tool to prove or disprove that. The tool was used to interrogate this previously unreportable bookings system and quickly identified customers who had visited sites on a frequent basis. We selected 1,000 of those customers and 1,000 at random (as per the previous process). We sent marketing literature out to both groups and then followed the results carefully. It wasn't a surprise when the group that we had selected using the BI tool as repeat customers had a six-fold improvement on engagement rates and a 100 per cent improvement on booking rates. This therefore told the CEO it was worth investing the money in building out this BI capability properly as there was tangible value to be had from it.

In terms of understanding the make-up of the customer base, again the business had a long-held belief that the most someone would travel to go to one of their sites was around two hours. However, utilizing a map-based visualization combined with customer data, we combined customer addresses and park locations. By selecting parks on the map, you could then see the postcodes from which the guests had started their journey, and in many cases it was more than two hours away.

RETAIL USING AN AI-BASED PREDICTIVE ANALYTICS SERVICE

This is a good example of the value a specialist data science business can provide. I worked with a firm that provided this specialist consulting service to large B2C business. I recall one example we looked at was for a notable film studio that produced movies. The film studio was keen to understand to what extent they could predict the dollar revenue generated at the opening weekend for any of their movies so as to have early indicators where things were not on track in order to rectify them in advance of launching. The team worked with the film studio to analyse multiple internal and external data sets and identify statistical correlations between data sets. This helped narrow down on those things that impacted most on opening weekends.

After much research they identified that there were a number of factors that contributed to this more than others. For example, one was that people were more likely to go to the cinema when the weather wasn't as hot. Another was the extent to which the movie was being talked about on social media in advance of its release and whether the chatter was positive, negative or ambivalent. To do this, the business used AI and mathematics to analyse huge volumes of social data and techniques such as NLP to determine the sentiment of each post. There were other factors in play, too, relating to the cast and genre of movie and so on. Using these different characteristics in various combinations and then testing them on prior data sets for their historic films, the team was able to develop a formula that combined these characteristics in just the right way in order to accurately predict the opening weekend takings for a given movie.

5.2.4 CHAPTER SUMMARY

- BI tools allow you to combine multiple data sets in order to create interactive dashboards and reports.
- These dashboards and reports can typically be created by business users and the interactive nature of them means

you can interrogate your data for insight without having to ask IT to write a new report each time.

- Whilst BI tools are generally used to refer to the front-end software tools business users will use to create these reports and dashboards, there are many components required to create a robust 'Business Intelligence' setup.

- These include raw data sources, tools to extract and transform these data sources, a database in which to store the outputs from the data and the BI tool itself.

- To get the most out of these tools you need to be clear on your value levers and the supporting data items that impact on those value levers. This should be used as a starting point to direct your focus on which parts of the data you really need to clean up and work with.

- Getting the data clean and matched up across multiple data sets is difficult but essential. This task is made much simpler if you have really honed in on the data you need.

- Note that different tools have different relative strengths and weaknesses – their suitability will in part be determined by what you need them for.

- If you want to take this a step further, work with a third-party specialist data science business that will be able to combine both the BI tools and technology with maths, statistics and predictive algorithms to really help you supercharge the insight you can get from your data.

5.3

ERP and PSA

5.3.1 OVERVIEW

Enterprise Resource Planning systems (ERP) are systems that are designed to manage the entire operations of a business in a single software application, from sales through to production, warehouse, accounting and the surrounding services and processes. Historically, ERP systems have been aimed at the manufacturing sector or businesses that deal with physical products. Professional Services Automation (PSA) is effectively an offshoot of ERP – taking the ERP concept and applying it to businesses that deal in professional services/projects. To understand these systems better and what they are capable of, I think it's worth me spending a little time explaining the history of these systems.

The concept started in the 1960s when Material Requirements Planning (MRP) came into being and combined previous paper-based approaches to production scheduling and inventory control with developments in computing technology. This focused on 'just in time' inventory principles and so the main areas of focus were inventory control, bills of materials (also known as BOMs – the list of components and quantities required to make any given product) and production scheduling.

In the 1980s, MRP II came along (changing its name to Manufacturing Resource Planning at the same time) and took MRP concepts a step further to encompass everything MRP I had covered, plus capacity management, forecasting demand, accounting and quality control. For the first time there were software programmes that could handle the end-to-end activities of the manufacturing and accounting side of the business in one single system and database. As the world and software evolved further this then expanded to include other aspects of the business such as CRM (customer relationship management), human resources and customer services, and out of that, systems that could handle the entire end-to-end activities of the business were developed, now called Enterprise Resource Planning systems.

Why is this history relevant? Understanding the evolution of these applications from the manufacturing sector is useful for two reasons:

1 It makes it easier to understand what is really at the core of these systems, i.e. why they exist and what sort of problems they were trying to solve;
2 It helps to demonstrate why there was a need for further iterations of these systems, such as professional services automation (PSA).

As you can see from the history above, the genesis for these systems was around efficient operations of a manufacturing business, and making sure that components were available when required and that there weren't unnecessary piles of inventory lying around (the real genesis for this was in fact the economic order quantity model designed back in the early 1900s – a mathematics and paper-based system). Whilst the concepts of these systems are good (who wouldn't want one system to efficiently oversee and manage all aspects of their business?), as noted they are really designed for businesses that deal in products rather than services. PSA – taking the principles and concepts behind ERP and attempting to apply them to service businesses (law firms, IT service firms, consulting firms etc.) – has evolved. As a result, it is less focused on physical inventory management, bills of materials and production scheduling and instead focused on 'resources' (i.e. people – who they are, when they are available, their capacity, areas of expertise etc.) and 'orders' (the projects or services that are being provided, the timelines and requirements for each one), and marrying up the two. They don't always incorporate a finance system within them and in those instances will usually integrate with whatever finance system you already have. This is simply because accounting for services businesses is generally much simpler than manufacturing – you have project or service revenue coming in and overhead and employee costs coming out. By contrast, in manufacturing businesses your costs are more complicated and management of the balance sheet and working capital is inextricably linked to inventory control and work in progress.

In truth, whilst ERPs are universally common systems, PSA is a concept that is more common in the US than the UK at present, albeit more and more firms are now looking at PSA seriously in the UK to help manage and organize their businesses. Since ERP is a more common system and generally more all-encompassing, we will use ERP as the basis for much of the content of this chapter, but I will incorporate comments and pointers on PSA where it makes sense to do so and where it differs from ERP.

So what are the core components and hallmarks of an ERP system?

One System to Rule Them All
The concept of a single database, a single source of the truth that can be utilized and accessed by different parts of the business for different purposes is core to ERP. The whole point of these systems is to get away from the disconnected nature of having multiple systems and spreadsheets to manage different parts of the business operations and the challenge that comes with then stitching those things together in an organized fashion. For example, consider a scenario in which you have customer orders coming through via an order system that isn't connected to anything else. Someone needs to take that order and then enter it into another spreadsheet or system so it can be analysed for production scheduling and inventory management (i.e. to make sure we have the bits to make that product and to decide when we have capacity to make it). If the inventory management system isn't then talking to the production scheduling system, it might not be obvious that a component or components required to produce the product are not yet available. In which case you won't find that out until manufacturing commences! The result: lots of half-finished products lying around that cost money to make

but can't yet be sold to generate income (unnecessary work in progress/WIP is not a good use of cash and this impacts value, as we know).

You can see how these disconnected data points also have room for error and how huge inefficiencies will creep in as the business grows, meaning you may need more and more people to keep the lines of communication flowing in the absence of systems and data to do that for you. It also makes reporting pretty painful. For example, how will you know at any given point (with any confidence) what is going to come out of the factory and how will you forecast cash and income coming in from clients if you can't be sure you will always complete on time the things you start? It also makes inventory control challenging – most manufacturing businesses will be familiar with the concepts of safety stock levels and reorder points – i.e. for any given component or product, what are the minimum stock levels required and at what point do you need to reorder them taking into account lead times etc. This works really well where you have accurate historic data and even better if you have accurate order forecasting. However, if neither of those are robust and you don't even trust the data you hold on existing inventory levels, it's almost impossible to do properly. The result will be inefficiency and either not enough stock (and no income!) or too much and therefore a drain on cash. You can see why a single system that connects these different elements of the process together with a trustworthy single source of data is going to make life a lot better for your business (more on that point on data later – it's pretty fundamental to this working properly).

Typical Functions

ERP systems do vary in some respects from system to system, but typically the below are the modules/functions you would expect to find in an ERP system:

- Customer and contact management
- Estimates and quotes
- Sales ordering
- Production (tickets and schedules)
- Procurement – managing purchase orders and inventory/stock levels
- Billing
- Accounting and finance
- Quality control
- Demand forecasting
- Customer service
- Human resources
- Reporting and dashboards

PSA systems differ slightly and tend to include:

- Customer and contact management
- Estimates and quotes
- Sales ordering
- Project management
- Document management (think statements of work, RFPs, project documentation etc.)
- Resource management (the people you have to perform the work, their skills, experience, level, capacity, working pattern, any particular skills of relevance such as language or qualifications etc.)

- Calendar
- Expenses and timesheets
- Interfaces with accounting systems and CRM systems (sometimes this is included, but for reasons described earlier less essential than for manufacturing- or product-based environments)
- Reporting and dashboards

Integration With Hardware

This is a concept more applicable to ERP systems than PSA and it relates to integration with other pieces of physical equipment that extend the capability of the software. For example, consider inventory management. With an out-of-the-box implementation of an ERP system, you will have records of each component in the system and stock levels for each one. As and when new stock is delivered it will need to be logged on the CRM system by someone in the 'stores' or department of materials, and then, as and when new orders go into production, the inventory is 'reserved' in the system for that particular order and then stock levels reduced once the order is marked as complete. Pretty efficient and simple to understand but it still relies on someone updating the system accordingly. On a periodic basis you will then do stocktakes to ensure that the figures held for inventory are correct. One extension that can make this process simpler are hand-held scanners so that as and when items are scanned this process automatically updates the system rather than needing to be typed in manually. You may also integrate with hardware that monitors the OEE (overall equipment effectiveness) for the machines in the factory to factor that into capacity planning, opportunity analysis and reporting.

How Can ERP and PSA Impact the Value Chain?

I've put ERP systems in the technology for profit and cash generation section of this book because in reality this is the value these systems can generate. However, it should be noted that whilst ERP is not going to help grow revenue in the same way a good salesforce system or online store might, it is pretty hard to grow either a services- or product-based business in a material way without something like this in place organizing the business. Where these systems aren't in place, it is not uncommon for the business to become increasingly disorganized and inefficient as it grows, which means senior management time is distracted with firefighting and fixing the day-to-day operations rather than focusing on clients and growing the business. This does then impact revenue.

High-growth businesses tend to have good people and also tend to be well organized with a strong system backbone.

Generally speaking, a good implementation of an ERP system can save cost through better utilization of resources and people – it can help you reduce the rate at which you need to hire more staff, particularly if you are growing your business quickly. It should also help reduce waste or failure demand by virtue of the fact you have one source of data rather than introducing the risks that arise when rekeying data between multiple systems.

Cash generation is also a key value opportunity with ERP systems and it can be created in a few ways. Firstly, inventory control. In an ideal world, you would order components required for products so that they arrive just in time for production to start, finish every product in the right amount of time and then ship off to the customer as soon as it's efficient to do so. This would reduce the need for a large warehouse and also reduce the need to spend cash on unnecessary inventory. Every component or product sitting in your warehouse without a product (order) waiting for it is wasted cash that you can't use to grow your business. It's trapped as either inventory or work in progress and that's not what you want. Clearly, what I have described is the ideal scenario and I am not suggesting this is typical of what you will expect to find or achieve every day. However, the closer you can get to that the better. It stands to reason therefore that any system that can help you more accurately manage your inventory will improve your cash position.

Likewise with billing and invoicing – ensuring that invoices are sent to customers once orders go out the door (i.e. goods out have marked the item/s as shipped) will help your collections and reduce your working capital requirement.

Similarly, with PSA systems resource management is also crucial. Let's assume that as you are running a services/ project-based business you are likely to employ individuals with sought-after or in-demand skill sets and therefore they are probably relatively expensive. It doesn't make sense to have individuals under-utilized or on the bench for too long as you are again covering the cost of them without the corresponding revenue coming in. Being able to more accurately schedule and manage resources so that their utilization rates are optimized is a strategy for creating value.

Before we go on to the specifics around how you can create value with these systems, I should also throw in a note of caution. ERP systems can be very complicated and costly to implement and there are plenty of studies that show many projects run over budget, over time and don't deliver the benefits expected. There are many reasons for this but most can be summed up by the concept that theory and real life often disagree and are often incompatible! ERP by definition is all-encompassing and as such designed around good/best practice. Trying to get this into businesses with very established ways of working that may be different to the design within the system is a big challenge. That doesn't mean you won't get value doing it and it doesn't mean you shouldn't try. After all, plenty of businesses do this and make it work. Businesses such as Amazon wouldn't exist without advanced systems that manage and organize every aspect of their business through technology. However, you do need to give these systems the healthy cynicism and respect they deserve; if you don't take an implementation of a system like this seriously – and by that I mean everyone in the firm from the top down – it is almost impossible to get real value from it (and you may even find you go backwards). Take your time to capture your requirements before making a software selection, try and get your businesses on a platform such as this before the growth kicks in as it's easier to do in a smaller setting, and as always start simple and expand.

5.3.2 HOW TO CREATE VALUE WITH THESE SYSTEMS

Understand Your REAL Objective and Value Opportunity

As with many of the chapters in this book, the first pointer here is to really identify what it is you want to achieve once you have implemented the system. You need more specific goals than 'I want to organize my business' or 'I want one system to improve my reporting and MI'. Of course, those things are important and who wouldn't want that (I've never met a CEO who told me he wants a disorganized business and to fly blind), but you need to get more specific. For example, if you say 'I want to better organize my business', then ask yourself why. Are you worried your business is becoming less profitable as you grow? Or are you worried being disorganized is meaning you aren't meeting customer demand fast enough? Or that being disorganized means you have to keep moving to bigger premises to store all your product and components? Or that your recruitment seems to be going through the roof but you aren't really sure what value these extra resources are adding? There are endless ways of drilling down into this question, but the point here is what are you really trying to get to – are you trying to increase profitability, and if so how? Or improve cash flow, and if so how?

You really need to get to a few critical objectives that are measurable and which tie back to the value levers we discussed at the start of this book. The reason for this is that, as you have hopefully gleaned so far, ERP and PSA systems are all-encompassing systems that impact every part of your business. It is impossible to get everything right across all departments and processes from the outset. As you go through the project you will need to make trade-offs and decisions to prioritize some things and de-prioritize others. Therefore, you have to be clear on your absolute end objectives so that each time you have to make a call on priorities or compromises, you don't accidently do something or decide something that will make that goal unattainable. I firmly believe (from my own experience and conversations with others) that the reasons these systems often fail to deliver the benefits they are expected to is because the business ends up seeing 'Implementing the ERP system' as the objective or measure of success rather than 'Reducing inventory by X' or 'Improving debtor days by Y' etc.

Spend some time, therefore, going through your business and thinking about where the real opportunities lie. To help you with this, here are just a few common opportunities you might want to consider and to give you some ideas as to how to think about this. Likewise, it can be helpful to draw the order to cash cycle in your business (the steps each order goes through, from order to cash in from customer, and how long it takes for something to get to the next step) and look at the areas where there is a particularly long delay.

1 Inventory control. We've talked about this a lot already so I shall try not to repeat too much here, but this is an obvious area to which you can add value. If you can better manage your inventory so the components or products you need are in place at the right time (without over-stocking) then you will optimize your inventory and improve your cash position;

2 Human resource management (and the cost of). Applies to both ERP and PSA but in a different way. In a product-based setting you want to ensure your people aren't replacements for systems. So, for example, it's perfectly sensible to employ people to work the machines, manage teams of people, work on assembly lines, work sales and support functions such as finance, HR, direct sales etc. What you want to avoid is employing people who are simply there because there is a need

to circumvent or micromanage processes in order to compensate for weaknesses in systems and data. For example, people who have all or part of their job rekeying information into more than one system, or those who are doing lots of 'checking' because you can't trust data. People who are employed to collect information on an ad hoc basis because the CEO or FD wants to know something and your MI simply isn't capable of providing it. This also applies to support staff – if your finance team are growing in number to keep on top of the invoices that need chasing, that's another sign ERP can help you;

3   In a PSA or project-based setting, it's about ensuring utilization of staff is optimized and you don't have an overly full bench. In the same way, you don't want zero capacity, as that will prevent you from growing. If you have poor data on utilization or your wage bill is going up faster than your revenue (and that wasn't your intention!) then that may indicate an opportunity for PSA to help you;

4   Improving collections/debtor days. You don't want to have to rely on the diligence of your finance team to issue invoices to customers or chase up when they don't pay! ERP systems know when products go out the door and as such are perfectly capable of issuing invoices. ERP systems also know when invoices remain unpaid and, again, can automate chasing overdue amounts.

Data, Data, Data

ERP success will live and die by the quality of its data. Without good data a successful ERP or PSA implementation is impossible. The point of ERP is that it is going to help you make decisions, manage processes and take action based on the information contained within it. For example, order stock when stock is low, manufacture something when it is due on the production schedule, assign something to the schedule once an order is created etc. If your data supporting these things is wrong, the outcomes will also be wrong. Chaos is a real possibility here.

In the case of PSA systems it could be you end up assigning people to a project who don't have the right skills, or double booking them and then looking foolish in front of clients when they either don't show up for a meeting at all or they show up but aren't capable of discussing the things the client wants to talk about.

It's essential that after identifying your goals, you get to work cleaning up your data as the next most important priority. In some businesses this will be easy. For most businesses this will be a daunting and fairly painful job. There are a few things you can do to help make this process a bit easier and I've tried to give you some suggestions as to how you can go about that below.

What types/categories of data do you really need to get right?
This is an important question to get right and to spend some time thinking about. It's pretty much impossible to clean up every item of data in every system and spreadsheet in your business. This is where the importance of properly and forensically identifying your real objectives comes in. If you know what you need to achieve, you can focus your efforts disproportionally on those data sets and the categories of data you

need in order to make that happen. For example, if your objective is to reduce inventory by £1m, then it wouldn't be a good use of your time to spend weeks or months cleaning up your customer data sets or HR records as they aren't going to impact materially on your inventory levels. Instead, you would focus all resources on getting starting inventory levels correct, ensuring your bills of materials are accurate, and your reorder points and safety stock levels have been properly calculated. You would then accept that if at launch there is a bit of duplication in the customer records for a few months until you've had a chance to sort them out, it's not the end of the world because you would be focusing your efforts on ensuring the inventory management elements of the system were really humming.

Likewise, you might decide for a PSA system that you don't need historic calendar data or projects and instead it's more important to focus on people's skills and qualifications, along with working hours, to ensure that the system is capable of assigning people to projects and will get it right.

How much of that data do you need?
Again, this is important to consider so that you avoid spending time cleaning data you don't need. How much history do you really need to carry over? In some cases lots, in other cases perhaps none. In the same way, consider the scope of data that needs to be cleansed. Take our example from a moment ago where our objective was to reduce inventory by £1m. Before going away to clean up every bill of material record and every safety stock and reorder point calculation, you might ask yourself the following: of the inventory you hold, does the 80/20

rule apply (80 per cent of the value is in 20 per cent of the products or components)? If so, you might be able to deliver £800k of the £1m target saving by focusing on that 20 per cent first (this is more common than you think!).

You can see that by using these sorts of questions we have narrowed down the data-cleansing task quite considerably from potentially every item of data in every spreadsheet and system in your business to a few categories and for a subset of the records, i.e. the top 20 per cent. Despite massively narrowing down the focus of our efforts, we haven't compromised the end objective because we were clear on that from the start and worked methodically through from there.

Process Review

As highlighted in Chapter 5.1 on process automation software, processes are rarely designed and more often than not evolve in order to deal with problems as they arise. Often, processes contain an element of people compensating for shortcomings in data or systems. ERP or PSA implementations offer you the chance to rework your processes to fit in with the system. Whilst you don't want to have 'the tail wagging the dog', the more you are able to adopt the out-of-the-box ways of working with the system and adapt your processes to suit it, the simpler your implementation is likely to be. These systems are engineered to link all parts of the system together in order to manage all aspects of the business efficiently. Customizing the way these systems work to a significant extent will make things harder, as you will then have to work through all the knock-on impacts of your customizations on the other parts of the system and workflows.

Training First

In traditional projects the process often goes something like this:

1 Define objectives
2 Scope requirements
3 System selection
4 Design
5 Build
6 Train testers
7 Test
8 Train users
9 Launch

I have often found that undertaking the training up front, i.e. once you have defined your objectives and selected a system but before you start work on anything, is very helpful. How often have you been involved in a project where huge efforts have been expended on building and designing a system – and as soon as you train people on it, many questions come up on why something is done a certain way or comments made that the way in which the system has been designed to do a specific task won't work. It's best to find these things out up front! Understanding how the system is designed to work out of the box is a great way of framing the rest of the work you then do on the project, as you can understand what you are working with and head off some of those issues that would otherwise be identified at the very end of the process. It doesn't have to be done as a formal 'training session' – a series of deep-dive product sessions would work well and allow you to focus on different parts of the system with different user groups.

Imagine if you and I met for the first time and I asked you for your opinion on how I needed to reconfigure my house in order to accommodate my growing family. Surely the first thing you would want to understand is what you had to work with – i.e. what does my house currently look like and how does it function right now – before you attempted to help me improve it (or at least I hope you would!). The same applies here – really understand what you have to work with out of the box before you then get started on adapting and implementing it.

Implement Incrementally

A common theme in this chapter is that the all-encompassing nature of these systems can lead to unrealistic expectations that 'everything' in the business has to be fixed or changed in one go. It's perfectly possible to do it in stages and, again using your objectives as your north star, work out the minimum set of modules or functions you need to deliver in order to gain benefits. Typically, with ERP most things touch finance and so starting with finance or incorporating it into whatever the first phase happens to be is generally very sensible.

Set the Right Tone

ERP or PSA systems are designed to be cross-department tools. Therefore, it is not possible to get them up and running without the support of all of those impacted. As with all change projects, the tone has to be set at the top and filter down, but it's even more important for this sort of project than many others that the inter-departmental collaboration and co-operation is strong. You can't have one team deciding they are going to use an ERP system for production scheduling if the team who take the orders aren't putting them into the system!

5.3.3 CASE STUDIES

HIGH-END FASHION RETAILER

The business in question is a manufacturer, retailer and distributer of high-end clothing. Several years ago it was operating a small number of stores in the UK and wanted to expand both physically and online, but it didn't have the systems in place to facilitate this. The existing systems consisted of spreadsheets, multiple 'point of sale' (in-store) systems and paper-based processes, with no over-arching technology.

They decided to implement an ERP system to provide the infrastructure to scale their business, as well as reducing some of the time required to undertake warehouse administration. The ERP system that was implemented had in-store point of sale capability, integrated with the company's website and had an element of warehouse automation including the use of hand-held scanners. As part of the up-front diligence process the company spent a lot of time choosing and selecting an appropriate third-party implementation partner and this choice is credited as one of the reasons the project was a success. They spent time with the implementation partner getting under the skin of existing processes, and importantly challenging themselves (and being challenged!) as to why they did things in a certain way. As a result they decided to adopt as much of the out-of-the-box 'leading best practices' as possible, rather than simply taking their existing processes and putting them into another system.

This decision to re-engineer processes, implement an integrated system and to really invest time in getting under the skin of their existing business allowed them to reduce the time it took to undertake administrative tasks considerably. For example, they reduced stocktaking time by more than 70 per cent once the new processes were launched. In addition, this provided the retailer with the technology and infrastructure to scale up, which has allowed them to open more stores in the UK, expand their online and international presence and also outsource some of the warehousing processes that were previously done in-house, without compromising the overall operation.

HOME LIGHTING PRODUCTS RETAILER

The team at this global online retailer used many disparate systems to service and fulfil orders from 14 different marketplaces, including Amazon, eBay and other websites, across multiple geographic locations. As a result, the company struggled to get the accurate and timely management information that they required to make business decisions, and the MI they did produce was time-intensive to create.

The business implemented an ERP system in order to better manage the 'basics' and drive general efficiency improvements such as invoicing and payments, as well as integrating and consolidating the data flows between their central hub and the various online marketplaces and third-party logistics providers. The business was very clear on its objectives and had a detailed specification written up front to identify the issues they faced operationally and therefore the capability the new system would need to have in order to resolve these. As a result they set out to resolve some very specific issues and successfully delivered on this just three months after project kick-off. Their MI has improved considerably as a result, as has the cost to produce it. The business now has real-time information around stock levels, shipments, inventory adjustments, stock validation and purchase orders, all of which has been automated.

5.3.4 CHAPTER SUMMARY

- ERP and PSA systems are designed to provide a single system capable of managing and organizing all aspects of a business.
- ERP systems focus on product-based businesses and PSA systems focus on service- or project-based businesses.
- These systems can have a meaningful and demonstrable impact on the P&L and are primarily focused on the profitability and cash elements of the financial statements.
- They are complicated and large systems to implement and as such it is inconceivable you will get through a project without compromising or changing scope along the way. Therefore, being crystal clear in your objectives is essential if you are to navigate these decisions without sacrificing the value creation opportunity.
- Data is critical to the success of the projects and whilst often a daunting task, can be made simpler by focusing on

those data sets you really need and only focusing on the quantity of data required in order to deliver value.

- Train on the system first to better understand the system you are working with.
- Setting the right tone from the top and inter-departmental co-operation are important.

5.4

The Cloud

5.4.1 OVERVIEW

The cloud is something that is talked about so often in IT that I have no doubt you have heard of it. You probably also understand it to a greater or lesser extent, but if you are reading this chapter it suggests you either want to understand more about it, or you would like to better understand how you can maximize its value opportunity. Rest assured, I shall do my best to meet both of these objectives along with how you can ensure a smooth (and practical) transition to it. It's also worth saying at this point that whilst pretty much every article and book on this subject will tell you that cloud adoption is a positive thing to aspire to, from a value creation perspective it's not always so black and white, and I'll cover more on that later.

This is also a chapter that due to its subject matter has the potential to get the most 'techie'. I do my utmost to avoid this at all times, but if I do stray into technical language it's only with good intentions – to try and help give everyday meaning to technical concepts so that you understand what they mean. I have no intention (or ability!) to turn you into technical experts.

The cloud is a widely understood concept but there are specifics and nuances to it that are worth explaining to ensure a full understanding of what it really means in practice.

At a conceptual level, the cloud is easiest explained as leasing versus owning outright. If you buy a car outright, it's yours and you own it. You have a big cash outlay up front, use the car for as long as it lasts, and over time you will need to buy new parts for it, have it serviced, pay someone to fix it when it breaks. Eventually, you will have to weigh up when it's just running too slowly or expensively to continue functioning usefully as your car and you will then have to replace it. Leasing a car, on the other hand, doesn't transfer ownership to you – simply a right to use it for a specific period. It involves little or no up-front payment, regular payments on an ongoing basis for the use of the car, and depending on your lease agreement, often the servicing and fixing costs are picked up as part of the agreement. At the end of the lease you give the car back and get something else.

In both of these options you have a car to drive and are paying something for it. However, the profile of payments is different and the 'hassle factor' is also different in that you have full responsibility for maintaining and looking after something you own outright as opposed to little or no responsibility to look after it if you lease.

The same applies to the concept of cloud computing. In days gone by (pre-commercial cloud), you would have purchased servers, a rack to put them in, a room in which to keep them secure and cool, lots of cables and related equipment to protect and link them together, and probably one or more individuals to maintain the equipment. This involved large cash payments up front for the hardware and then ongoing operational expense for small incidental items (things you can't capitalize or depreciate) and for the salaries of the folks looking after them. You also had to think about disaster recovery, backup and security – both electronic and physical (how do I stop someone hacking into this and how do I stop someone breaking into my office and walking out with it!). I am using the past tense here, as although these days are long gone the reality is many businesses still operate in part or in full like this and for a variety of reasons. So if that's you, you aren't alone.

Cloud computing works differently to this. Instead of purchasing the servers, racks, room, cables etc. yourself, you let someone else worry about that, for example Microsoft or Amazon. You then rent some of their computing power – to use as a file server (network drive) or for storage, for example – and pay for what you use. For the day-to-day user there is little difference. For example, if in the old model you would have logged on to your computer and then clicked on one of your network drives to access the company filing system, the same setup on a cloud infrastructure would look and operate exactly the same way. It's just that when you access a file, instead of the request from your computer being sent to the server room next door, it's being sent to the server room in whatever data centre your cloud provider is using.

What's different? Well you haven't had to purchase and set up any particular equipment and you aren't worrying about securing the servers physically (let's assume you've gone with a cloud services provider like Microsoft who obviously secure their data centres with some pretty impressive defences). You don't need people to maintain the equipment either. You do, however, still have to worry about cyber security and you do still need someone to help you configure and optimize/monitor your cloud environment. Now that might not be a full-time job (or it might be many full-time jobs depending on the size of your business) but there is still a need for a technical/skilled person in this.

There are other benefits too – for example, if you need to run a piece of software, either for a limited time or permanently, that requires a particularly specific and high-spec setup (for example, an AI application or data-analysis system). You don't necessarily want the time or expense likely to be required to build and configure a high-spec bespoke piece of computing equipment – much simpler just to rent it from someone who can spare the power and have it up and running in minutes.

There are different types of cloud computing models and then different types of cloud services. I've summarized these below. Before we get into this, however, there is a concept called 'virtualization', which is worth understanding at a superficial level just so that you understand a bit better how the cloud works and what you are 'really' renting.

In the traditional model, you would purchase a server and then access that server from your computer. If you needed a new server you would purchase another one and then access that from your computer too. However, over time people realized that this was pretty inefficient. For example, if one server was temporarily under strain and needed more computing resources you would have to purchase more RAM for it. Even so, the server sitting next to it might be operating at 50 per cent utilization and so you actually have enough RAM between the servers – just not in the right proportions at that given moment in time. The same applied to disk space. Technology therefore evolved to allow the separation of the software part of the servers (the bit you as an end user actually use) from the physical hardware that they operate from in a process called virtualization; in other words, creating virtual servers that looked, felt and worked like normal servers but that weren't specifically tied to one specific piece of hardware. That way the real physical resources (disk space, RAM etc.) could be shared between the 'virtual servers' as and when required, which made for a far more efficient use of resources. Why do I mention this? Simply because this is an important concept in understanding cloud computing. What you are renting or leasing from a cloud services provider is often not a physical piece of kit but a virtual server/computer running on several different pieces of physical hardware. Therefore, when considering cloud computing don't think you are necessarily renting a physical server – it's almost always the virtual equivalent.

Public Cloud

A public cloud provider manages and maintains physical computing resources (servers, file storage etc.) and then offers them as a service to businesses to consume as required via the Internet. As explained above, you are renting virtual servers or space from them and for that reason, setting up a new 'server' or increasing disk space can take a matter of seconds. Likewise they can be shut down or decreased in power or specification at the drop of a hat because it doesn't require a physical change in any kit – just a change in the amount of resources allocated to the virtual server.

Advantages of this model are that the whole setup is very flexible, simple to get going and truly a 'pay as you go' model. It allows you to benefit from the cost efficiencies promised by cloud providers since you are using it largely as designed (out of the box) and only paying for what you need. In their simplest/purest form, security is typically easy to implement with a good provider since it's a dedicated environment, ring-fenced (albeit virtually), and as such the cloud providers are able to design out-of-the-box security setups with this in mind (they don't have to take into account interactions or integration with any equipment that isn't their own). They simply secure the physical kit, protect your data – usually encrypting – and provide you with a secure mechanism with which to access it.

The downside is that it is a pure cloud adoption model and, as such, can be complicated for older businesses with old equipment or systems to migrate to.

Private Cloud
This is pretty much the same technology as the public cloud in terms of using virtualization to pool physical resources to support virtual servers, but it refers to physical resources that are not shared. With a public cloud, as per the example above, whilst your virtual servers are yours and separated from other companies' servers on the same kit using software, you are sharing the physical pieces of kit/hardware with other firms who are using the same cloud provider. In a private cloud the physical hardware is yours and yours alone. Often, these types of cloud are run in-house, i.e. within businesses premises, but some can be done with external data centres in what is known as a 'co location' model (your kit, someone else's premises).

The advantages of a private cloud can be responsiveness (in theory, if located in your offices then access to the server is not dependent on the Internet connection speed) and security, since your equipment is not being shared (although I am not sure I agree with this for smaller businesses from a physical security perspective – I would challenge any assertion that the majority of small- or medium-sized businesses can run a more secure data centre than Microsoft or Amazon can afford to). The downsides are that it can be more expensive because the physical resources are not shared, and if they are located within your premises (rather than using infrastructure in someone else's data centre) you still own the kit and have to service and maintain it.

Hybrid Cloud

A hybrid cloud environment is a mix of public and private clouds, i.e. mixing some on-premises cloud technology with public cloud technology. This is the case for a variety of reasons – for example, you could decide to put non-essential services in the public cloud and mission-critical/time-sensitive services in the private cloud. If you chose to do this by design, i.e. having fully costed and assessed the financial and operational benefits of this model and decided that is the way to go, then well done, carry on. However, many businesses operate a hybrid cloud not by design but simply because they are midway through a migration to the public cloud model and as such can't decommission old equipment but at the same time are paying for public cloud services. In this particular case, it's probably the worst place to be both financially and operationally. Why? Simply because you can't get the benefit of the savings you would if fully on a public cloud model, and you are paying cash every month to rent it whilst also paying larger amounts of cash to maintain physical equipment you own and the people needed to support both. As I said, if you have designed a hybrid cloud model and it's the most sensible and cost-effective for you then that's one thing, but being in this situation by accident (as many businesses are) is not ideal.

Generally speaking, running costs for public cloud models offer the best savings potential versus traditional models, private clouds less, and hybrids somewhere in the middle or sometimes even no savings at all (if, as I said, not by design).

Alongside the different cloud models we have looked at above, there are also services (products) based upon the cloud computing model and these are described below.

Infrastructure as a Service (IaaS)
Infrastructure as a service is the most fundamental level of cloud computing services – i.e. you rent the IT infrastructure (virtual machines, storage etc.) from a cloud provider and usually on a pay-as-you-go basis.

Platform as a Service (PaaS)
This is the next level up from infrastructure as a service and includes the environments required to build, test and deploy software applications. It is designed to allow developers to build applications quickly without having to set up the infrastructure below it to run their applications, thus focusing all their time and efforts on building software and not configuring and fine-tuning hardware.

Software as a Service (SaaS)
This is another level up again and the most common way you will come across cloud computing. These are software applications that run in the cloud and you simply sign up and start using software rather than having to download, install and configure. There are lots of examples of this out there in the business world – Salesforce.com, Hubspot, Microsoft 365 etc. Even a basic tool such as Gmail is effectively providing you with software as a service – in this case an online email management software platform.

Hopefully you are still with me, not overloaded with technical jargon, and ready to understand how you can generate and maximize value using cloud computing technology. If so, please read on...

5.4.2 HOW TO CREATE VALUE WITH CLOUD COMPUTING
Whilst I hope you are excited about the opportunities cloud computing can bring to your business, the value creation potential depends a lot on your setup, business model and the extent to which the pros and cons of cloud computing align with your business priorities. Here are some of the things to consider before diving in.

Financial Impact
Important and often overlooked is the way in which you account for the cost of cloud services versus traditional hardware and IT. This can be a real determining factor in whether cloud is good for your value creation. (There are other reasons to do things besides simply to make money, but this book is focused on value creation, hence the way we look at these things will be

focused more on shareholder value creation in the traditional, i.e. monetary, sense.)

Traditional hardware has an up-front cash payment, referred to in most companies as CapEx (capital expenditure), which is recorded on the balance sheet and is then depreciated over its useful life in the P&L. Therefore, the impact on cash is significant, but the impact on EBITDA is zero, and the impact on EBIT or PBT is reduced – especially in later years if the kit is fully depreciated and you are still using it.

However, cloud computing has no up-front cash cost but does feature as an operating expense on a monthly basis. It does therefore impact EBITDA (and EBIT and PBT) but also doesn't get any cheaper on an annual basis as you are permanently renting rather than depreciating.

This means that if you are cash tight and focused on cash generation as a means of creating value, cloud computing can be very beneficial. However, if you are very focused on EBITDA then cloud computing can often be financially worse than the traditional model. This of course is not the full picture, as what we aren't considering here is the cost of employees in both scenarios, and if you have a team of people maintaining hardware that you can reduce down to one individual by moving to the cloud, then you will generate EBITDA savings via the headcount reduction. If, however, that isn't the case and let's say you have the same number of people before and after, or the people cost savings aren't enough to offset the increase in operational expenditure on the cloud services, you need to have a think about whether this makes sense financially. To illustrate the point, below is a worked example showing two scenarios.

EXAMPLE 1

Scenario A = Hardware purchased up front for £50k and depreciated over 3 years then replaced in year 4. Assumes 2 staff required to support infrastructure on £50k each

Scenario B = Public cloud infrastructure as a service model for £12k per annum, supported by 1 IT staff member on £50k

Scenario A: Traditional model	Y1	Y2	Y3	Y4	TOTAL
Cash Cost of equipment	£ (50,000)	£ -	£ -	£ (50,000)	£ (100,000)
Staff Cost	£ (100,000)	£ (100,000)	£ (100,000)	£ (100,000)	£ (400,000)
EBITDA Impact	£ (100,000)	£ (100,000)	£ (100,000)	£ (100,000)	£ (400,000)
Depreciation	£ (16,667)	£ (16,667)	£ (16,667)	£ (16,667)	£ (66,667)
EBIT Impact	£ (116,667)	£ (116,667)	£ (116,667)	£ (116,667)	£ (466,667)

Scenario B: Cloud model	Y1	Y2	Y3	Y4	TOTAL
Infrastructure Cash Cost (operating expense not capex)	£ (12,000)	£ (12,000)	£ (12,000)	£ (12,000)	£ (48,000)
Staff Cost	£ (50,000)	£ (50,000)	£ (50,000)	£ (50,000)	£ (200,000)
EBITDA Impact	£ (62,000)	£ (62,000)	£ (62,000)	£ (62,000)	£ (248,000)
Depreciation	£ -	£ -	£ -	£ -	£
EBIT Impact	£ (62,000)	£ (62,000)	£ (62,000)	£ (62,000)	£ (248,000)

EXAMPLE 2

Scenario A = Hardware purchased up front for £50k and depreciated over 3 years. Assumes 1 IT Staff on £50k

Scenario B = Public cloud infrastructure as a service model, £12k year 1 rising to £15k per annum supported by 1 IT staff member on £50k

Scenario A: Traditional model	Y1	Y2	Y3	Y4	TOTAL
Cash Cost of equipment	£ (50,000)	£ -	£ -	£ -	£ (50,000)
Staff Cost	£ (50,000)	£ (50,000)	£ (50,000)	£ (50,000)	£ (200,000)
EBITDA Impact	£ (50,000)	£ (50,000)	£ (50,000)	£ (50,000)	£ (200,000)
Depreciation	£ (16,667)	£ (16,667)	£ (16,667)	£ -	£ (50,000)
EBIT Impact	£ (66,667)	£ (66,667)	£ (66,667)	£ (50,000)	£ (250,000)

Scenario B: Cloud model	Y1	Y2	Y3	Y4	
Infrastructure Cash Cost (operating expense not capex)	£ (12,000)	£ (15,000)	£ (15,000)	£ (15,000)	£ (57,000)
Staff Cost	£ (50,000)	£ (50,000)	£ (50,000)	£ (50,000)	£ (200,000)
EBITDA Impact	£ (62,000)	£ (65,000)	£ (65,000)	£ (65,000)	£ (257,000)
Depreciation	£ -	£ -	£ -	£ -	£ -
EBIT Impact	£ (62,000)	£ (65,000)	£ (65,000)	£ (65,000)	£ (257,000)

In Example 1, scenario A shows the equipment purchased in year one and replaced in year four, supported by two individuals. This is compared to scenario B in which the cloud is used and the staff are reduced from two to one FTE. You can see in this example that scenario A requires £100k of cash to purchase equipment over the four years and the EBITDA impact is -£100k per annum owing to the staff cost. The EBIT impact also takes into account the depreciation of the equipment and hence is -£117k per annum. Scenario B, however, has no big up-front cash cost as you are renting the equipment and since it is a simpler outsourced model assumes you only need one staff member, meaning staff costs are halved. As a result, the cash impact is lower and also the EBITDA impact is -£62k per annum. This is an example where the finances work and there is a benefit to moving to a cloud model as whether you are valuing on a multiple of EBITDA, EBIT or even taking into account cash, you will be better off with the cloud model/ scenario B.

However, consider Example 2. This isn't that much of a stretch from Example 1 – all we are changing here is an assumption that in year four the equipment still works so we don't need to purchase any more, and that in both scenarios the staffing requirement is the same.

Suddenly the case for cloud computing (on a purely accounting basis) is harder to make.

Scenario A, the traditional model, has a total EBITDA impact of -£200k over the period and total EBIT over the period of -£250k.

Scenario B, on the other hand, shows a total EBITDA and EBIT impact over the period of -£257k and a higher cash cost for the infrastructure vs the cost to purchase it outright. In this example therefore if you were valuing on a multiple of EBITDA EBIT or even taking into account cash, you will be better off with the traditional model in scenario A.

All the above is trying to show you is that you shouldn't take it for granted you will be automatically financially better off with a cloud model. It comes down to multiple factors – whether cash is a priority over operating profit, what the specifics of the different models actually mean when you run them through a financial model as we have done above, and whether there are other savings such as staff costs or premises costs and so on that need to be factored in. Model and appraise the options carefully before simply assuming cloud = savings.

Connectivity

As noted previously, the public cloud model works on the assumption your infrastructure is located somewhere outside the office (e.g. in a Microsoft, Amazon or Google data centre) and you therefore access your virtual servers via the Internet. If you have a fast connection and a good secondary line (backup Internet line) then you're going to be fine. However, if you are in a part of the country where the speed is poor or you don't have resilience via a secondary line then you need to think a little more carefully about how much you will be impacted if the speeds are slow. It's also important to consider this if you are thinking about a hybrid cloud model in which servers in your office will need to talk to servers in the cloud. For those processes that rely on that communication between your offices and cloud servers – you can only go as fast as the slowest point in the chain.

Related to connectivity but more specifically speed, is that if you have mission critical applications that require absolute speed then you may also consider public cloud to not be appropriate. An example might be algorithmic stock trading systems in which milliseconds can make a difference in pricing and as such any delay at all can be costly.

Decide Where You Will Get the Greatest Benefit
If you have run the scenarios and models and decided the cloud is for you, you then need to work out where you are going to get the greatest benefit. Is it in moving the infrastructure the company needs on a day-to-day basis into the cloud (infrastructure as a service) or is it more about adopting software as a service (applications that run in the cloud). For example, let's say you currently run an old SAGE accounting system on an in-house server and you decide it will be financially and operationally beneficial to move to the cloud. Rather than renting a server from Microsoft or Amazon on which to install SAGE, you might simply decide it's simpler to pay SAGE for its own cloud-hosted version of the software.

Integration of SaaS Systems
One of the big challenges with cloud – particularly when you start to adopt software as service applications from different vendors – is how you then integrate these systems, which you have little to no control over or access to, with the configuration and 'back end' of them.

For example, consider this: in a traditional setup where all applications are installed on your servers, if you want to extract some data from your CRM system and feed it into a data warehouse or perhaps your finance system, your IT folks should in theory have access to all the databases they need to make this happen. Yes, it requires investment, time and expertise, but the point is it is possible to do this because you control all the bits required to make it happen. If you rely on SaaS products, you are seldom granted access to the underlying databases. At best you will be given the ability to connect to the data using APIs and if not perhaps only be able to extract the data via the in-built reporting tools. In this example, connecting data from different systems together can be very hard. Now, of course many software vendors are aware of this and do offer APIs, but you still need expertise to access them and you will need somewhere to store and join up the data you extract. There are some very good cloud integration tools to purchase that come with out-of-the-box plugins to lots of the well-known SaaS platforms like Salesforce, Office 365 etc. The point of this isn't to dissuade you from using SaaS software, but simply to point out that if you need to do something with your data beyond putting it into whatever SaaS system you are considering, check first that you will have access to the data in a format with which you can do something useful!

Consider What You Really Need to Have Round-the-clock Access To

One of the benefits of cloud computing is that it is on demand – therefore you need to decide what you really need access to 24/7, what you need access to during work hours and what you need access to only when you need it (i.e. ad hoc). For example, if you don't need to access your file servers outside work hours, set up your virtual servers to power down at 7pm and power back up at, say, 8am. That way you aren't paying to use computing power when you don't need it. Likewise, we all have archives of data we need to store either for regulatory purposes or just in case we need to refer to it, but that we don't need access to on a regular basis. You could consider storing this data on a much lower-spec server or in a compressed format when not in use and then only changing that when you need to access it. These sorts of techniques can make a big difference to your monthly cost.

Even for those servers you use on a regular basis, don't feel the need to get them overly specified up front. It's not like you are buying something outright that you need to last for several years; if you set up a virtual cloud server and subsequently find out you need more space or power – you can just adjust it on the fly. Don't pay for what you don't need!

Geography

Location is a pretty important consideration, particularly in relation to the legal aspects of doing businesses. Some laws, for example GDPR, place a requirement on you to store your data in certain territories and not others. This can impact the cost and efficiency of cloud services. If you are a business with a reasonable international presence, you may need to ensure that your chosen cloud provider can offer you data locations in the territories you require.

Having the Right People

It's important you have the right people on hand to help you a) transition to the cloud and b) make the most of it going forward. Moving to the cloud can be a very complicated and costly business and firms with complicated or ageing infrastructure should consider working with a specialist partner who can oversee and manage the design and implementation of your cloud strategy.

In the same way, security arrangements may need to differ and adapt for a cloud environment, and the value of specialist support in this area is not to be underestimated. Don't assume that your security setup in-house will translate into the cloud environment – often it won't be sufficient.

You need to consider whether you have the right people in-house to help you assess this opportunity and manage it going forward. It's not a given that the people who are right to set up and maintain an in-house IT setup are the right people to help you manage and optimize a cloud environment.

5.4.3 CASE STUDY

FINANCIAL SERVICES BUSINESS

I have worked with a financial services business that moved its entire infrastructure into the cloud. This meant Office 365 for email and productivity software, SaaS systems for things like CRM and finance software, and leased 'pay as you go' servers for services such as file storage. The business engaged a dedicated cyber security firm to support in the design of the cloud security setup, to ensure appropriate monitoring and protection combined with the benefits of remote access for staff, for example a VPN to enable staff to work from home.

The benefits to the business were that the internal costs to oversee and manage this infrastructure were low, with no full-time IT staff employed. The business could also grow quickly without having to worry about the IT equipment keeping pace. This was true for a number of acquisitions made by the business, since the nature of the infrastructure allowed the firm to migrate new firms on to its infrastructure within weeks rather than the months or years it would typically take. This was essential in getting value from the acquired businesses as quickly as possible and operating the combined businesses as one. A drawback to this setup was access to data on SaaS systems and so time was invested in integrating the APIs in critical SaaS systems with other applications stored on databases maintained by the business itself (albeit these servers were still cloud-based).

5.4.4 CHAPTER SUMMARY

- The cloud has provided businesses with an alternative 'leased' model for the use of servers and infrastructure.
- In the case of public cloud, rather than purchasing equipment yourself, you simply rent from firms that offer this service via the Internet.
- In the case of private cloud, the servers are dedicated to you but virtualization software still provides some of the benefits you would expect from the public cloud.
- A hybrid cloud is the use of both public and private cloud models. When done in a considered fashion that has determined it really is the best model for your business, this can create value. However, if you have arrived there by accident then you need to look at this option carefully if you want to avoid unnecessary expense.
- You can purchase different products (services) based upon the cloud – ranging from basic infrastructure as a service all the way through to software as a service.
- Accounting for cloud services versus traditional hardware purchases is different and you need to carefully model the impact on your financial statements before committing.

Understanding up front if you place more value on cash or EBITDA (or EBIT) as a route to value creation is important in guiding your decision.

- Connectivity is a key consideration, too, as poor Internet performance can kill a cloud implementation.

- When using SaaS systems, try and identify up front what you need to achieve from a reporting perspective and whether it can do this for you. Also enquire as to how you can access your data in a more raw format should you want to carry out your own reporting or combine with other business data.

- Cloud is a different model and so don't be afraid to change the way you operate to get the benefits from it. For example, shutting down servers when not in use, not over-specifying servers up front etc.

- Geography can cause challenges from a legal perspective – choose a cloud services provider that offers you control over the location of your data.

5.5

Collaboration Technology

5.5.1 OVERVIEW

Technology has without question fundamentally changed the way businesses operate – we've talked about a number of examples of this already and there are many more examples still. Technology has also changed the way we – people – operate, and it's changed that more rapidly than it has businesses. It's changed the way we consume news, the way in which we see technology as a natural and everyday extension to pretty much everything we do and, most importantly, it's changed the way we communicate.

The challenge for business is that it's impossible for business practices and processes to evolve at the pace with which personal technology and personal technology habits evolve. For example, in our personal lives we regularly use phone-based video conferencing to communicate or collaborate (how many times have you jumped on a quick FaceTime call in order to better explain something to a friend that is easier shown than described?). Likewise, we regularly utilize technology to quickly combine and triangulate multiple data sources in order to answer questions quickly and as accurately as possible. An example might be discussing with friends where to go for dinner. With our personal technology we can quickly review all restaurants in an area, and having chosen one or two options we then look up reviews to see if they are any good and then check table availability. We might then even use a maps application to get us there or a taxi-hailing app to organize a ride. You don't even have to be in the same room as your friends to co-ordinate all of this.

The point is we are used to combining data from multiple sources quickly in order to make decisions, and having communication technology to organize everything in our personal lives – so used to it that we get frustrated when we can't replicate the same experience in our professional lives.

In a business context, this can be a harder experience to replicate for a variety of reasons. For example, when you jump into a meeting room at work and someone asks a question, do you instantly have access to the multiple data sources you need to answer the question? Or if turns out someone specific has that information, can you quickly conference them in via video to explain what you want? Most would say no, I suspect – and that isn't a criticism, just a reality of the pace at which personal technology and personal habits diverge from what is practical in a business context.

Now I should say that this is a very interesting time to be writing about this subject. I wrote the first draft of this chapter when nobody had heard of COVID-19 and yet as I came back to do a review of the chapter as part of the editing process several months later, we were into global lockdown. This technology is now more critical than ever.

Much of what I had written before needed to be updated – either because it had predicted ways of working in the future that have since come to pass or because the pandemic was driving further advances in these areas as I wrote that will create further opportunities for businesses to collaborate through technology. Incidentally, this also serves to make two important points – the first being that this technology is fundamental to a business in terms of both competitive advantage and resilience, and the second simply the pace at which technology can fundamentally change the way we work.

Collaboration technology in the workplace is seeking to overcome that divide and help us work more productively and flexibly at work. This can and will have many profound implications – both positive and negative – for businesses today and an even greater impact on the shape of the workforce and working patterns in the future. Already, services like VPN software and mobile computing have allowed people to work from home as part of the normal course of business – something that simply wasn't commonplace even say 15 years ago. Whilst no one can predict the future, as a result of the advances in these technologies and as was demonstrated in early 2020 in the midst of a global pandemic, it isn't hard to see greater flexibility, much less dependence on a fixed office location and more multi-location teams becoming a dominant and common feature of many businesses in the next decade and beyond. I am certain, as are many others, that the workplace of the future will look and operate in a very different way to that we have been used to and whilst I don't believe that we will never return to working together in offices again as some have predicted, I do believe the future workplace will have far more fluidity to it and certainly the technology will continue to adapt to support this.

Whilst these collaboration tools can play a supporting role in the delivery of products or services to clients, they are usually not the product or service itself (unless you happen to run a collaboration technology business) and therefore they are about helping you work more efficiently and at a lower cost rather than growing revenue or about helping you deliver your services through another more efficient/cost-effective channel – hence the focus here being on technology for profitability rather than revenue growth.

There are a number of different types of collaboration technologies you can utilize and they can be differentiated in a number of ways. I am going to look at some of them and from the perspective of either real-time or non-real-time tools.

Non-real-time Collaboration

These technologies are designed to help you collaborate more efficiently with colleagues, often when they are not in the same physical location. However, these are described as 'non-real-time' tools because they allow you to each work independently on your various contributions to whatever it is you are doing and then the technology brings it all together. This is very useful when working on things that are either linear processes, where you have different teams working on different aspects of the same project, or where working hours across team members are not compatible (either due to shift patterns or perhaps international considerations, for instance). Examples of these sorts of technologies are:

Document collaboration

Software applications like SharePoint or Google Docs allow you to collaborate with colleagues on a single master file from different locations and at different times. For instance, you might have a presentation you need to complete for a pitch and you and colleagues each have specific slides you need to update. Rather that each updating a different version of the presentation and then having to send round to each other for feedback and to pull into a master version, you can all work in the same document – at the same time – and see the changes you have made and others are making in order to quickly produce a single presentation. Note this isn't the same thing as saving a PowerPoint presentation in a location on a network drive and all using that – whilst good practice, you may still find yourself limited to one editor at a time. I am referring to software here that allows concurrent editing by multiple people.

Project or task collaboration

Task-management and project-based tools can help teams collaborate on particular projects or activities with visibility on the status of everyone else's tasks. By way of illustration, you may have a process in your organization for reviewing and signing off sales pitches. It might be as simple as a sales manager completes, the pitch is reviewed by a peer and it is then signed off by the sales director, finance director and operations director. Tools such as Asana (also covered under process-management tools, see page 126) can help teams organize process or projects into tasks, assign them, and then upload documents, comments and status updates against them so all involved can see where things are.

This is also commonly seen in software development environments where working with distributed teams across many different geographies is common. Tools such as Trello help organize tasks (like requirements or features) into different buckets, such as 'to be reviewed' 'waiting for development', 'in development', 'ready for testing' and 'released'. These can be managed as 'cards' under headings and then each card dragged under the next heading in the workflow at the appropriate point – a bit like a kanban system. These cards can also contain a lot more information that you can build up over time. By way of example, you might have an entry that says, 'Build the login screen'. Someone responsible for reviewing new features might select that 'card', open it up and, noting that it needs more information, put a couple of comments in it asking for certain information for the product specialist. That specialist can then open the card and answer the questions. Once the original reviewer is satisfied the question has been answered the card might get moved into the 'waiting for development' column. Each morning the developer ready for his/her next task will pick up the next item in the queue – in this case our login screen – review the information entered against the card and the full history of the discussion is available to read. Likewise, they can ask any questions before completing the work and moving it into test. The tester picks up the next card in the list and again has the full history in the tool to learn from before undertaking their role testing the login feature etc. Whilst a very specific use case, this has much wider application than technology and I've seen tools and processes like this work very well across pretty much every sort of project you can think of, from software to websites to organizing complicated events and even to managing a pipeline of potential financial investments.

Knowledge management

Knowledge-management tools are certainly not new and yet still surprisingly under-utilized within most businesses. At the simplest level these can be 'one-way' communication tools – such as the classic company intranet designed to communicate information within the company to all staff but which is protected from the public eye. More advanced or collaborative implementations are two-way, meaning a variety of teams and individuals within the business can update or amend their sections, thus allowing teams to create their own individual knowledge hubs. This can be for general team communications; it could also be used for process or policy sharing, 'how-to style guides' etc. Tools such as SharePoint have been around a long time and can be very useful in that regard. There are also several versions of Wiki technologies you can implement in the business if you want an internal company 'Wikipedia' (although SharePoint also does this very well too).

Time and diary management

These tools are fairly self-explanatory and are designed to help teams manage diaries and timing for tasks, projects and so forth on a collaborative basis. These are often components of the project or task-management software as described above.

Real-time Collaboration

Whiteboarding

Whiteboarding tools are, as you would expect from the name, designed to replace the traditional whiteboard with dedicated digital versions. They may sound a little clichéd but the reality is for distributed teams trying to work on something together that requires visual support, it's often not a good use of time (or practical) to have someone work up all the visual aids nicely in advance or create PowerPoint slides on the fly. Sometimes you need to just pick up a pen (digital pen) and start scribbling whilst discussing with colleagues. My suggestion with these tools is the simpler the better – if the purpose is to try and recreate the free-flowing and sometimes more intimate nature of conversations you would traditionally have with a flipchart or whiteboard in the room, you want to be spending all your time doing this and not on operating the technology!

Video conferencing

This is well known to everyone (particularly now!) so I won't spend a great deal of time explaining. What I will do is point out that there are more options available now than historically – from single-use video-conferencing rooms you can sign up for on the fly through to more comprehensive tools such as Microsoft Teams that allow you to screen share, video conference and work across multiple devices. Almost all work across laptops, desktops, tablets and mobiles, so don't settle for anything less. If you are a Microsoft house then Teams comes as part of some Office 365 subscriptions and it is worth checking whether that applies to you before you spend too much money on something else. At the time of writing, Zoom and Teams appear to be the dominant forces – but I have no doubt given the importance now and in the future of video conferencing we should expect to see these tools develop at a far greater pace in terms of reliability and functionality than seen previously. As one example, I fully expect Virtual Reality to make its way more into the mainstream of these sorts of technologies soon to help put people 'in the room' and facilitate closer simulated social interaction.

Instant messaging and internal social media
There are many examples of these tools – too many to mention them all here – but the idea behind them and their role in productivity is to foster a more informal channel for communication between colleagues, thus speeding up the process of getting things done. Emails can still be seen as very formal and because of this individuals often spend as much time re-reading and re-writing them to ensure the tone, content and positioning are correct before they hit 'send' as they do writing them in the first place. Social tools and instant messaging are generally seen as more informal and therefore people generally feel more comfortable firing off a message on the platform quickly and more directly than they do via email. As such, you can potentially cut down on time wasted writing and perfecting emails and get on with acting upon the information shared. They can also have a positive cultural impact, making written communication between colleagues less formal and in the process breaking down some of the barriers emails can often create. (Be honest – how many times have you received a short email from someone that ends with the word 'Regards'

and you've spent more time than you should wondering if that means 'Wishing you well' or 'Politely bugger off and stop wasting my time'!)

5.5.2 CREATING VALUE FROM COLLABORATION TECHNOLOGY

Objectives

As always, starting with your objectives is important. Collaboration software can be used in a variety of ways and whilst books like this can provide ideas as to how you might get value from it, only you can identify the area(s) of your business on which this can have the biggest impact. There are ways in which you can appraise your business and determine which of these tools might be the most appropriate. Considering the following aspects can be helpful:

Multi-location

The extent to which you have teams across multiple locations will in part determine some of the tools that will help you create value. For example, if your entire business is based in one location and unable to work from home, whiteboarding software and video conferencing are unlikely to be particularly useful tools! However, if you do have teams across multiple locations then you might consider if you could save time, travel costs, or simply make working between office locations simpler with the use of such technology. For instance, if you do have a business with multiple offices, do you ever find yourself saying things like 'OK let's discuss that next time John is in London' or 'OK let's make time to go down and see Sue and discuss this properly'? If so, you are delaying decisions and conversations based on your ability to converse with someone in a more intimate or personal manner than phone calls or emails allow. Whilst waiting until you are literally sitting in front of the individual might be the right thing to do in some instances, in many cases you could be introducing unnecessary inefficiency into your business and that is the time to consider if these technologies can help. In these cases, you might measure reduction in travel costs or a reduction in the number of days staff spend travelling as evidence/KPIs you are adding real value with these tools. I expect many of you have experienced this anyway during the pandemic and these conversations and ways of communicating will be second nature to us all when we go back to an office environment (whatever that looks like). It's also worth noting these technologies can also help reduce the geographic hiring barrier. For example, with remote working and locations, your pool of potential employees is no longer relative to your office but any individual on the planet with the right skills and experience and who speaks your language (possibly also in a similar time zone but that will depend on the work).

Availability of information

If folks in your business spend a lot of time asking people how to do things, where something is kept, where they can find something (digitally) or 'Do we have a policy for X' and so on, then it's a pretty safe bet there are opportunities to use the above tools here. Specifically, this is where the knowledge-management systems can come in useful – ensuring you have a single source of truth rather than many policies and procedures can save a lot more time than you think. Not to mention the improvements you will see to quality of output if people are all following the same processes or procedures (and the correct version of them).

Existing working practices

Thinking about what you currently have in the way of collaborative technologies or working practices may help you identify areas in which these tools can improve what you currently do. For example, if you have monthly briefings for all staff via conference call you might consider video conference an improvement on that. Are you a document-heavy business – for example are you regularly producing responses to RFPs or customer proposals and are these currently managed via email and with multiple versions of the same document flying around? If so, document collaboration might improve working practices here by reducing error and time spent collating different inputs into a single final document. You can quantify the benefit here in a number of ways – two of the most common would either be in terms of hours saved (efficiency) or in reduction in the cost of mistakes. That is to say, if you put sales proposals together and they have inaccurate figures in them, this could cause you to lose the opportunity or to under-quote for it, meaning your margins are reduced. If this is a trend or particular issue you have identified in your business, you might set yourself a goal of reducing material errors by say 25 per cent with a tool such as this, which gives you all a specific goal to work towards.

Internal or External

One of the considerations you need to give to these technologies if you are to get value from them is to be clear on whether these are internal or external tools. If you are going to be using these tools to collaborate with clients and therefore introduce these technologies into your product or service delivery, you will consider different aspects of the selection and implementation to be more important. For instance, if it is to feature in communication with clients (regular meetings, brain-storming sessions, idea sharing etc.) it will need to be a) easy to use, b) integrate seamlessly with the rest of your delivery tools and c) require nothing complicated (or at all) to be installed at the client end. If you can provide a very slick and simple technology interface to clients, arguably this can be a selling point or USP. The opposite is sadly also true – get it wrong, pick tools that are difficult to use, or require your clients to spend hours on the phone with their IT department to get them to work – and it could end up making you look unprofessional and perhaps less efficient in your clients' eyes. At the time of writing most businesses are working with an element of grace all round – i.e. it's accepted we're all dealing with the challenges of working from home and that we all have to 'make do'. As such, when the technology fails or doesn't offer a seam-less experience, I'd like to think we are all pretty forgiving. However, once it is possible to return to a normal working environment then expectations will also rise and there will be less room for forgiveness if you continue to provide a poor technology experience to clients in this way.

Culture
Undoubtedly one of the more challenging and non-technical issues to overcome is one of culture. If you work in a business

with a workforce that is relatively tech savvy and open to new ways of working then you will have a different set of cultural challenges to those that aren't. If you are in a business where you don't have a high rate of tech adoption and/or there is a high degree of scepticism for these sorts of technologies, short of mandating that everyone use whatever collaboration technology you want to introduce, you will need to take people on the journey with you. This is likely to involve one of two things – either starting small with a group of the least resistant and proving the value in practice, or alternatively starting with your biggest problem and addressing it that way. Even the most cynical individual will struggle to justify a negative stance towards something like video conferencing, for example, if you can demonstrate it is going to save you tens of thousands of pounds a year in travel costs. Interestingly, you might think that in the opposite culture type (tech savvy and happy to try new things) you won't have any issues, but you would be wrong! You get a different sort of problem – one of technology proliferation. That is to say, you have a situation where everyone is so keen to find an app or software programme to solve every problem that you can end up with multiple video-conferencing solutions, different document-management platforms per team, a combination of instant messaging, email and internal social media in use, and all this comes with its own challenges. For example, if your communications are spread over multiple systems how do you satisfy GDPR requirements that each platform has been carefully vetted with the right contractual arrangements in place and that you are comfortable the data is appropriately protected (and that you can get to it if you need to satisfy something like a subject access request)? Likewise, improving processes can be hard when each team has a different system or combination of tools they are working with.

Complexity to Set Up

Referenced to some degree in the sections above, it is worth ensuring whatever solution you pick is relatively simple to set up (i.e. don't assume that all modern tools that claim to be easy to set up and use really are – give them a go and find out yourself). You don't want to lose 10 minutes at the start of every meeting setting up the video-conferencing or whiteboarding software – otherwise you may soon find your simplest route to efficiency gains in the future will simply be to switch off the technology! This will be particularly important when we do return to an office environment and you are then mixing business-grade infrastructure and technology with home working setups. Getting that to work smoothly may be harder than we realize.

Privacy and Security

As I reference in the cloud technology chapter (5.4), big technology firms will have resources in place to protect and safeguard data and information in a way that you almost certainly won't. However, as you will also know, the weakest link in any corporate firewall these days remains your staff and as such even the most sophisticated systems can be undone from a security perspective if you have users who aren't securing passwords or are susceptible to phishing attacks. Clearly, the more technologies/providers you have, the more systems you need to monitor and protect with things like two-factor authentication in order to give yourself peace of mind that the information is secure. You will also need to consider privacy laws and applicability to your firm – for example, in UK and Europe GDPR is a big feature of privacy regulations and as such will require contracts with technology providers to cover specific data-protection points and to provide safeguarding for any data held outside the EU. This is something you will need to confirm with any technology you choose that hosts data in the cloud – and collaboration technology is no exception.

5.5.3 CASE STUDY

BUILDING A SOFTWARE SYSTEM ACROSS LOCATIONS

I once worked in London on the build of a software system, but the team I worked with were all in disparate locations. We had a project manager in a different part of the city, a couple of programmers in the north of England, a designer who worked from home several days a week, and subject matter experts in various other home locations around the UK including Scotland. It was a software project and was run as an 'agile' project – meaning we worked in two-week 'sprints' and each sprint would see several features built, tested and released from start to finish. The project was then built up over, say, seven to eight sprints and meant that every two weeks you had an updated working version of the product, each version with more features than the last. Each sprint would have a typical pattern to it – a meeting lasting several hours ahead of the start of each sprint to agree what was going to be delivered in the next two weeks; daily 'stand-ups' for 15 minutes at the start of each day to check in on progress, commit to the deliverables for the day and clear any blockers; and then retrospectives at the end of the sprint to look back and share learnings based on what went well and what didn't in order to improve working practices ahead of the next sprint.

Now, you can imagine how all these things work pretty easily in practice when everyone is in the same room – when spread around the country as we were, the only option was to use technology to collaborate. For example, for our daily stand-ups we would use video-conferencing software and someone would share their screen either to demo the previous day's work or to show the latest version of the sprint board so we could see who was doing what that day and what still had to be done. For our planning meetings we would use a combination of video conferencing and screen sharing to run through requirements, and whiteboarding software for our retrospectives to quickly get down on paper our views on what went well and what didn't so we could discuss as a team and agree actions. As and when ad hoc issues arose during any given day, we would just jump on a video conference, look at the problem together and as a result quickly unblock any issues.

This was a very successful project and delivered on time and under-budget. What was also interesting was the camaraderie that developed over that period; team bond was as strong as for any team I have worked in despite the fact we had never met each other in person. When we finally got together for drinks to celebrate delivery of the project many months later, it was like catching up with old friends. The reality is there would have been no economical way to deliver this project with those people and yet they were the absolute perfect team for the job. The collaboration technology meant we didn't have to compromise on the people we used, nor did it need to impact the efficiency with which we operated.

5.5.4 CHAPTER SUMMARY

- Collaboration technology has and will continue to change the way businesses operate and connect with staff, clients and partners.
- Collaboration technology can provide productivity improvements, efficiency gains and cost savings through travel and expenses.
- The technology can also play a role in helping you hire and retain the best people, since with a good collaboration infrastructure it shouldn't matter where staff are located, which means your pool of potential talent is far greater than it might have been traditionally.
- Collaboration technology can involve real-time interaction such as video conferencing and whiteboarding; it can also involve non-real-time interaction such as document collaboration, knowledge management and project and task management.
- Applicability will vary from business to business and depend on a number of factors, including whether you are spread across multiple locations, where your biggest

challenges lie with your existing communications technology, and the nature of your interactions with clients.

- Culture plays an important role in adoption and both
'tech-adverse' and 'tech-embracing' cultures can create
challenges. Therefore, you need to be cognisant of the
culture you have and the problems to watch out for.

6

Project Management

The first few chapters of this book were focused on defining what we mean by delivering value through technology, specifically what we mean by the term 'value', and then the subsequent sections have been focused on the various technologies you can look to utilize if you want to create that value in your business. However, it isn't simply enough to be clear on what we mean by value and then to identify one or two technologies that are capable of delivering it. It's also critical to ensure you manage the process of implementing your chosen technology solutions well and this is the focus of this final section – project management.

I have deliberately taken a slightly broader and therefore looser definition of 'project management' for the purposes of this chapter and have incorporated aspects of investment appraisal and change management too. In this chapter, we will explore what we mean by project management and the various phases or components of it, we will look at some of the more common methodologies, what they mean and when they can be most effective, and we'll also cover some of the pitfalls to avoid along the way.

If you enjoy the subject matter covered in this section and want to delve into any of these areas in more detail, you will find a wealth of books, articles, websites and courses devoted to these subjects available to you. As with all the chapters in this book, I'm not trying to make you a better project manager here, but just help you to understand what these different techniques and methodologies are so that you can ask better questions of the people you appoint to run projects and are aware of what to watch out for.

Project-management methodologies can be split broadly into two groups: 1) those that are sequential and considered more traditional methodologies and 2) those that are iterative and are considered more modern approaches. However, you shouldn't read this as traditional = bad/less effective and modern = good. Both have merits and challenges and some are more suited to certain types of projects than others. It's going to be more about how well you implement and leverage your chosen approach than anything else, although naturally certain methodologies will better suit certain types of projects and we'll cover that too in our assessment of each one.

As the name suggests, a sequential or 'traditional' methodology tends to organize projects into distinct phases that take you from idea, appraisal through to design, build, test and implementation in that order, with one phase generally finishing before the next commences. As a result, much of the documentation, thinking and design is done up front before any building work begins. These projects also tend to involve more-detailed contractual negotiation up front with the focus being on delivering the defined and agreed elements of the project for specific commercial terms.

They are relatively intensive from a project-management resourcing perspective, i.e. they need to be tightly managed and generally work best where the requirements and solutions are well understood early on and the requirements are unlikely to change materially. This approach can be useful in forcing people to think through processes or requirements in great detail up front and getting the specification articulated in great detail before any money is spent on technical resource. As a result, you also typically find at the end of the project you have far more comprehensive documentation since this was required to get to the build phase. It's also a highly logical approach on the face of it and as such it's pretty easy for most people involved in the project to get their heads around it and understand what's going on and what stage a project is at. (This isn't so true with the more iterative approaches.)

There are of course several downsides to these sequential approaches. The first is that people often don't know what they really want until they see something/play with it and in a sequential or waterfall approach this can be quite an issue as you don't tend to get to the testing phase until right at the end of the project. This is one of the reasons that these sorts of projects overrun or overspend. It can also be quite hard to build momentum in these projects, as generally people get excited about what they can see and touch rather than concepts and, again, that part of the project happens right at the back end.

The iterative approaches to project management generally tend to focus on multiple short iterations (a bit like mini projects) within the overall project and each iteration is designed to deliver something tangible at the end. These iterations can be weeks in length or perhaps up to a month but rarely longer than that. The specific methodology you use (more on that in a minute) will determine exactly how the time in each of these iterations is structured and organized – it can look a little disorganized or chaotic to someone new to it, but my experience of these approaches is that when done properly they are very regimented and have a very strong framework around them. The positives associated with this approach are that you see working product very quickly and this is good for two reasons. Firstly, you reduce the risk that you spend ages building something that people don't like or that doesn't do the job, as your end users have plenty of regular opportunities to test and refine the product as it develops. Secondly, it's also good as it really helps build up momentum and belief in a project. The downside to these methodologies is that they really do need to be run by people who know what they are doing. They are perhaps less intuitive for someone who has never done it this way before and the risk is (and I have seen this many more times than I can count) people just decide it sounds like a good way to do things quickly – no need for documentation up front, just 'build as they go' and see what happens but without properly adopting the structures and frameworks required to do it well.

WATERFALL PROJECT MANAGEMENT

Waterfall project management is a sequential project-manage-ment approach as described above, which means each phase is usually required to be completed before you can move on to the next. When implementing technology projects, the typical phases the project will go through are as follows:

Problem Identification

This is the stage in the project where you identify what problem it is you are trying to solve.

'Problem' may seem like an odd choice of word but it's essentially just a way of articulating what it is you are ultimately trying to achieve. If you think back to the ERP chapter (5.3) by way of an example, problems we were trying to solve there were reducing stock days or improving debtor days. In the case of the website project (see pages 175–77) it might be increasing the conversion rate etc. Whatever it is, you identify this up front and the rest of the project is then designed to solve that problem/deliver on that opportunity. A business case is usually built around this problem setting out the cost benefit analysis and we will look at that in more detail towards the end of the chapter.

Requirements Gathering

This is a pretty chunky part of these types of project as all requirements are documented in detail in order to make the subsequent stages possible. The requirements document is usually used to create test plans, design documents and as the basis for operational documentation, and as such it's important to get right. It's usually pulled together by a 'business analyst' and involves individuals from across the business who all feed into it to ensure it accurately captures the requirements from across the firm.

In smaller organizations and smaller projects this may just be a spreadsheet with all the requirements logged; typically in bigger businesses it is a Word document with more information on the project in it and the requirements are either referenced within or written directly into it. Typically, this document will focus on both functional and non-functional requirements. A functional requirement might be the ability to reset your password if you forget it, whereas a non-functional requirement might be that the screen should load in less than two seconds or that the site should only operate on HTTP etc.

Each requirement will usually be set out in a good level of detail, including any business rules, assumptions and exceptions. There is also some way of indicating the priority of the requirement, a MoSCoW approach, for example, breaks requirements into **Must**, **Should**, **Could** and **Won't Have**. That way if difficult decisions need to be taken later there is a mechanism for ensuring the priority requirements are understood.

You should expect the requirements document to go through many iterations and a thorough review process before it is signed off. If you are asked to review one of these things and you've not been in the detail (as is typical with most CEOs and MDs in smaller businesses), being presented with a document of this magnitude can often be pretty overwhelming. After all, you're reading this thing because you are trying to make sure things have been captured correctly, nothing has been missed and the requirement has been correctly articulated. After you've read 50 or more pages of requirements you can often come away feeling what can possibly be missing/what can you possibly add to that!

I've often found myself in this position and I've developed a technique I use to help review these documents and which you might find useful. This technique is something you have to really do before you start reading the document or it doesn't work properly. It's pretty simple and akin to the thought process I encourage you to go through in every chapter in this book when considering value levers in your business – grab a few blank sheets of paper and write at the top how you are expecting this project to help you add value to the business (of course feel free to use the appropriate chapter and examples in this book to help you do this). A few bullets or scribbles is fine – the simpler the better.

Then, in plain English, write down what you, as someone with no real prior knowledge of the project, would expect this particular system or technology to do for you, i.e. brainstorm your own list of requirements. It doesn't matter in what order you put them down and you will certainly miss things (that's OK). Give yourself a bit of time on this so at the end you look at the paper and in your own mind you're happy it's a reasonable reflection of what you think this system should do. Then open up the requirements doc and go through and tick off the requirements on your list accordingly.

What I usually find with this approach is that because you've approached it fresh, with good overall knowledge of the business, not hindered by weeks or months of requirements gathering, and you are applying a fresh pair of eyes, you will invariably spot things on your list that aren't in the document. Don't worry that the requirements document will almost certainly contain lots that you haven't thought of – this is why you hire people whose job it is to go through these documents cover to cover! The danger with reading it first and then trying to spot what's been missed is that you are then trying to take in so much information, process it, organize and apply your own mental model to it all at once, that you invariably miss things. Best to approach it fresh in your own way and then use that to compare the other document to.

Design

Once you are happy with the requirements document it's then time to move on to design. There are usually a few elements to this; depending on the project, these can be:

- Technical design
- Functional design
- Visual design
- Architectural design

In big projects, each of these documents will often go through several iterations from high level design (HDD) to detailed design (DD), whereas in simpler projects they are all in one document.

In reality, aside from the visual design most of these documents are for the benefit of the folks building the system and as such most CEOs and MDs will have little value add at this stage.

Build

This is exactly what it sounds like – configuring or building the product as per the specifications developed during the previous stages. This is largely a technical exercise notwithstanding it requires careful monitoring and managing during the process to ensure there is a clear view on progress versus timetable, and costs are being tightly controlled during this process. During this period the testing team are also often engaged to start building up the testing plans and test scripts. These are usually based on the requirements documents to ensure coverage in the test plan of the requirements. It's good practice to have a separate team working on the test plans to the build of the system to ensure the tests are written based on requirements and not necessarily on what has been built.

Testing

Testing is often broken into a least two stages – technical testing and user testing. Technical testing is usually undertaken by a tester with a good knowledge of how the system should work or how systems in general operate and where they often go wrong. The purpose of this test is to ensure it meets the requirements technically, i.e. it does all the things it is supposed to and doesn't have any 'unintended features' (bugs!). In software projects for which you are developing the software yourself, your developers can build tests into the code itself to automate some of this testing. Don't underestimate the time this will take going back and forth with the technical and build teams to get things fixed.

Once that's done you then have user testing. User testing is the opportunity to have the system tested by individuals from the business who will be using it on a day-to-day basis. They shouldn't really be testing if the system 'works' (as that should be picked up in technical testing); they should be testing with a view to ensuring that the system will actually work in the business practically, i.e. what we have built actually is fit for purpose, going to solve whatever problems it was meant to and is easy to use/compatible with the way jobs are carried out etc. All too often projects rush into this phase with many technical issues still outstanding and users get frustrated or, worse, lose faith testing the system because they end up just finding bugs and raising technical problems rather than thinking about how it practically works within the business. This is quite an effective way to kill a project – you'd be amazed the damage it does if the first experience with the new system is particularly bad – those individuals go back and tell everyone how terrible it is, how it doesn't work, and then all faith in it is shot before you have even started to roll out. Good luck turning that tide of momentum!

Implementation
Implementation is about getting the system live and into the business and people trained, ready to use it. Depending on the technology you are implementing then this phase will differ quite a bit. However, generally you will be expecting to see the team focused on any number of the below:

1 Communications
2 Training
3 Pilots/go-live dates
4 Final data migrations
5 Process updates

Again, if you are thinking about the areas in which you can add value/should be focusing on with a fresh pair of eyes, think about the things in my list above. When you have a stressed project manager in month nine of a six-month project trying to get a system tested and passed – negotiating between designers, builders, testers and users – they are often stretched in many directions. Often, so much is focused on actually getting those things done that some, like updated process documents, communications and so on can slip by the wayside. Those are the factors to look out for and areas in which you can add value as a leader.

PEOPLE AND GOVERNANCE

So what sorts of people are typically involved in projects like this? As you can imagine it will vary depending on the size of project and the technology you are implementing, but typically you would have:

- Business analyst
- Project manager
- QA/testing manager
- Development team lead
- Development/technical team (depending on what sort of technology we are talking about)
- Business champions/reps/testers

This might seem like a lot, but it's a pretty involved process and important you have experienced people in these roles. From a governance perspective it will again vary, but typically you might have weekly project team meetings that are attended by the project team and then perhaps monthly steering-group meetings to review overall progress, attended by perhaps the CEO, FD, COO and project manager.

Documentation is a big feature of these projects and that's also true of the governance arrangements; expect RAID logs (risks actions issues dependencies), status update papers, project plans, budget reports, to name a few.

AGILE PROJECT MANAGEMENT

Agile project management is an example of an iterative project-management approach and it differs from the waterfall approach in almost all respects. The starting point is the same – i.e. you still need to identify the problem you are trying to solve or opportunity you want to unlock. From that point on, things differ considerably. It's worth saying there are different versions of Agile methodology, such as Scrum, Lean, Extreme Programming (XP), kanban… the list goes on. This isn't a book about Agile and as such we will focus here on Scrum as an example as it's pretty common and a good example of Agile. The general principals and approaches are pretty similar through all of these methodologies and therefore as an introduction to Agile, Scrum will be sufficient.

As I noted above, this isn't a sequential process like waterfall and is iterative in nature. The diagram on p.231 gives an idea of how it works – we'll then cover these things in more detail below.

Product Backlog

The product backlog is the list of all the requirements for the end product, maintained and prioritized by the product owner (more on that role later). Each item in the backlog typically has a level of detail behind it described in 'user stories'. The backlog is the ultimate reference point for what will get done in the project – if it isn't in the backlog it doesn't happen! However, it is not usually required that you have all these items worked out in great detail up front; in most cases the requirements will just be listed out at a high level so as to get placeholders in the backlog and then

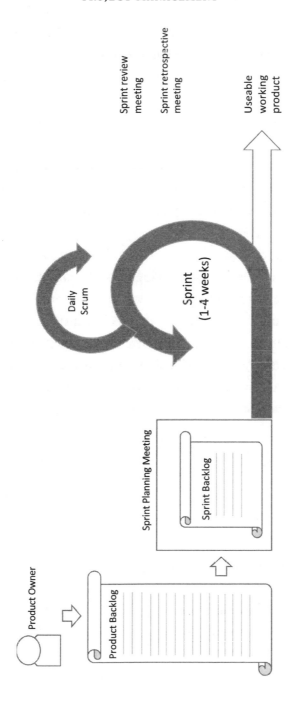

the detail is filled in by the product owner, typically at least one sprint cycle before they are required. The backlog items are sets of requirements or 'goals' on behalf of the users of the software. This means the user stories are typically broken down to a granular level of detail and typically written in the following format:

As a _____ I want to _____ so that _____

So, for example, you might have something like:

<u>Login requirement:</u>
As a registered user **I want to** log in to the system **so that** I can start using it securely.

You would then have more detailed acceptance criteria – and often multiple criteria that help the technical teams understand what is really meant by this and what would be an acceptable solution. Acceptance criteria is usually written in the following format:

Given_____ when_____ then_____

To continue our example, the acceptance criteria for this backlog item might be:

- **Given** I am on the login screen, **when** I look at the screen **then** I can see:
  - A username box
  - A password box
  - A submit button
  - A forgot password button

- **Given** I am on the login screen, **when** I enter my username into the box **then** the system checks that I have entered a valid email address;
- **Given** I am on the login screen, **when** I enter my password into the password box **then** I can see ** as I type instead of the characters I type, to protect the security of my password;
- **Given** I am on the login screen, **when** I click on the submit button **then** the system will check my login credentials and log me in if they are valid and take me to the home page.

Now, I could continue writing probably another four or five acceptance criteria for different scenarios, for example if the password is wrong, if I forget it, if I click the button and haven't typed anything in etc., but I hope you get the idea. It might seem like a lot of detail, but my experience is that because things are broken down to a low level and you are writing in very simple terms, it's actually much easier to write these than more traditional specifications as seen in waterfall approaches.

All items in the backlog eventually get put into this level of detail if they are to be worked on.

Estimating
Estimating in agile methodologies is typically not carried out using any form of conventional measurement such as hours or days. Instead, a points system is used – it can be something like a Fibonacci series (0, 0.5, 1, 2, 3, 5, 8, 13, 20, 40, 100), T-shirt sizes (x-small, small, medium, large etc.), or anything that gives you some form of quantifiable relative measurement.

This may sound counterintuitive, but it actually works well as it's often hard to estimate in real-time terms how long something will take and so a better system is to try and estimate something relative to something else. Therefore, when a project starts the team have to agree which system they will use to estimate and what the control or benchmark level is going to be. For example (and I am going to use the Fibonacci series here as I think it works well) you pick a task everyone has a good understanding of in terms of complexity and time to develop and then agree whether that task represents a '1' or a '2', and so on. For instance, you might pick 'adding a button to a screen' as the benchmark task and give it a value of '1 point'. Then each other task can be estimated in relative terms as to how much more difficult or time-consuming it is compared to the benchmark task you chose. For example, you might then estimate that writing the code to save a piece of text is going to take three times as long as the benchmark task – as such it gets 3 points. How does this ultimately translate into anything useful? Simple – over time, as each sprint goes by you will soon see how many points a team can deliver in two weeks, and as time continues that becomes a more and more accurate indicator of the team's capacity and output. You then know that, for example, two weeks may equate to the delivery of 30 points, and as such if you look at the product backlog and think it's probably about 120 points' worth of work, then you know based on the velocity of the team it will likely take another eight weeks to complete it. I hope I haven't lost you at this point. I promise if it sounds unusual and unnecessarily complex it really isn't – it works very well once you get a few sprints behind you and you can see the true capacity of the team.

'The Sprint'

To make sense of the other meetings and items in the diagram on page 231 you need to understand the structure of a sprint. A sprint is typically two weeks in length, but it can be one week and usually not more than four. At the start of each sprint you have a sprint-planning meeting. This is an important meeting, ahead of which the product owner should have organized the product backlog into order of priority.

In the sprint-planning meeting, the team take a requirement off the top of the backlog, discuss it, estimate the amount of time that it will take to build (in points) and then add it to the sprint backlog – the list of things to be built in the next sprint. The team will know the capacity, i.e. how many points they can typically get through in a sprint, and so will keep going through the product backlog until they hit their capacity. Then the sprint backlog is locked down and the sprint begins.

Each day, the team starts with a brief daily 'Scrum' (15 minutes is usual). This is a meeting used to plan and synchronize work for the next 24 hours – it's also for the individuals to commit to what they will deliver from the sprint backlog by this time the following day. It is not a status meeting – the focus is on who is going to do what, ensuring the team are properly co-ordinated and unblocking any issues. As the sprint progresses the backlog will get developed and the onus is then on the product owner to make sure these features then get tested and signed off. 'Done' means developed, tested and signed off.

Towards the end of the sprint, the product owner will ensure the next set of items in the product backlog will be ready for the next sprint. At the end of the sprint, the team have a sprint review where they demonstrate the working, tested and signed-off features to the users and each other. The team then have a separate sprint review where the team look at what went well, what didn't go so well and how they can take those learnings into the next sprint. This is also an opportunity to look at the velocity of the team (are the team getting through more or less points in a sprint over time) and then assessing the product backlog against that velocity. They then start all over again with the next sprint-planning meeting.

As you can see from the above, it's all highly organized and co-ordinated and as such if someone doesn't pull their weight or do their job then it soon starts to lose momentum and efficiency. In particular, it is demanding of the product owner and any testers who need to get things tested and turned around in a tight timeframe.

People

As you can probably tell by now, there are a couple of important roles beyond the development team worth highlighting:

Product owner – The product owner is the individual responsible for the set of requirements and therefore for maintaining and prioritizing the product backlog. Therefore, this individual needs to be highly in tune with the needs of the business, its priorities, and have sufficient time to devote to the process on an ongoing basis.

Scrum master – the Scrum master is responsible for managing the processes associated with the team, such as the daily Scrum meetings, sprint retrospectives, sprint reviews etc.

I have been in so many businesses that have heard of Agile, like the sound of it and decide to 'give it a go'. Please bring in individuals with real experience in this area if you decide to go down this road – it's not worth trying to do this without it.

INVESTMENT APPRAISAL IN BOTH MODELS

Investment appraisal is fundamental to whatever project-management methodology you use and as I alluded to at the start, I've given an overview of two different models above, but if you google this subject you will find there are many varieties and other models you can use (but these, in my mind, are the two prominent approaches). However, the need to get investment appraisal right is critical whichever you choose.

The first point to consider here is whether your business actually has a formalized process for doing this at the moment or not. If you do, then great, read the below in the context of appraising your existing process. If you don't, you should put something together in order to address these points.

Setting a template for investment appraisal is a good idea – give yourself a way to review requests to spend money on a comparable basis and allow you to review one against another. If everyone is allowed to come up with their own format, it's much harder for you to work out what you are supposed to be reading into each one or to be sure that when comparing competing projects for limited resources you are comparing like for like.

There are then three really critical factors in this process and the third of these in particular is the one where, in my experience, some firms get it wrong.

Firstly, financial returns – I have found in smaller businesses it's easier to ask the teams to present a breakdown on a cash-flow basis – cash out and in broken down into a reasonable level of detail. I would then typically ask the FD to review these and present to you based on the firm's accounting policies what this actually means from a P&L/financial statements perspective. This in my mind is preferable to asking your teams to get that right – i.e. don't ask them to assess the P&L impact but get them to set out the information you need and then you can do that yourself. You will be looking for an assessment of payback, IRR and NPV of cash flows.

Secondly, alignment with group strategic objectives. If you set out strategic objectives that could be annual targets – three-year plan, five-year plan, something else – then it's up to individuals to factor those in and think about them when recommending something for investment. Think about the earlier chapters of this book when we talked about aligning business strategy with technology strategy, and the chapter on value creation for further ideas.

Finally, <u>when</u> you assess is critical. Many waterfall projects in particular make the mistake of conducting the investment appraisal process up front, that is to say the first step is often a presentation of the business case in terms of costs and benefits and then very often businesses make a decision to proceed or not at this point. This is counter-intuitive if you think about the amount of work that happens after this stage. My suggestion would be to have several points a project needs to go through before approving final budgets when using the waterfall method.

It can be hard when working with third parties, who generally want to sign a contract up front, to then undertake all these phases from design through to delivery (again more of a problem for small than bigger businesses – owing to the types of partner you will be working with and the way the commercials typically work). However, it's worth giving yourself the opportunity to do this and working with a third party prepared to agree the commercials on this basis. How often have you heard people complaining about projects that overrun or cost more than expected? Often, that's seen as a failure of the project manager or project team to manage the project properly, but in reality, it's often setting expectations on how long something should take or how much something should cost way too early in the process that's the real problem!

Now, this works differently in agile for a couple of reasons. Firstly, since every sprint is designed to give you a working product at the end of it, and the process is based around working in order of priority, in theory you can stop at the end of any sprint and use whatever has been delivered at that point. However, in practice that's not always possible – particularly very early on in a project where in reality very little may have been delivered. Nevertheless, it does at least allow you to look at the investment appraisal in a different way, since you can agree a fixed amount you are able to commit to a project up front and then simply say that when you have spent that nothing else from the product backlog is going to get done.

Secondly, because you don't carry out a big requirements and specification process up front, it can be harder to estimate up front. There is a school of thought amongst the more hard-liner agile purists that says trying to estimate the cost and time associated with doing an agile project up front runs counter to the agile process. However, this book isn't aimed at them, and

I can say in my experience it's pretty normal to get an approximate estimate up front so you understand the quantum you are looking at. Just keep in mind your most useful control in that methodology is the ability to reprioritize every sprint, i.e. every two weeks, and if you are doing it properly then you will have a working product you can do something with every two weeks, too.

7

Conclusion

In the introduction to this book, I said that I wanted to provide you with a meaningful understanding of technology and its real value potential within businesses, and in particular, to understand how to apply developments in technology to familiar business principles such as revenues, profit, cash and valuation.

We have subsequently looked at various topics in a deliberate order designed to take us from the macro subjects such as 'What do we mean by value?' through to application of this to technology and business strategy, before then applying this thinking at a micro level to different sorts of technology.

I hope that you now have a firmer framework in your mind for evaluating and assessing technology investments in the context of your own business and plenty of ideas as to the technologies you can look to in order to create value and specifically, for each one, how you can unlock that value.

Whilst distilling an entire book down to a small number of key takeaways is always going to be a challenge, I would summarize the important things to keep in your mind going forward in order to create value from technology as:

- Understand what 'value' means to your business, this is the most important point. What are you ultimately trying to create and how do you value that?
- Understand your business strategy in relation to the value you want to create, unpick the key operational drivers of that value, and then spend time overlaying technology in the context of that;
- Recognize that different technologies impact different parts of the value chain and so if you are clear on how you want to create value and your business strategy for doing so, this can help narrow down the areas on which you need to focus your attention from a technology perspective;
- When assessing the merits of any particular investment in technology, don't try and debate the merits of it with technical people using technical terms. Bring it back to business basics. If you can't articulate the impact that this technology will have on the value levers of the business and how it will do that, it isn't worth spending the time trying to understand the technical stuff!
- Don't be led purely by trends – technology fads come and go – some stay and some don't. The only way you can really separate the worthwhile from the worthless is by relaying any technology back to its value to your business. Use the 'So What' test; i.e. why should you care about it?
- Once you have set out your technology roadmap and the investments you plan to make, you can then, for each one,

refer to some of the tips and suggestions in this book for how to get the most out of them;

- You will also need to ensure you have the right project-management approach in place to ensure a successful delivery – noting that different scenarios require a different approach.

To that end, I hope that above all else, if you take one thing away from this book it is that with a high degree of logical thinking and a good grasp of business principles, you can clearly link investments in technology to real, tangible shareholder value creation without needing to be a technology expert – simply by asking the right questions. And if you can do that repeatedly and deliver value as a result, you can rest assured you will be in an elite group.

ACKNOWLEDGEMENTS

There are many people I need to thank for their help and input, though I am sure I will forget some people and if I do it's not intentional.

I'd like to thank those kind individuals who gave up their time to support, review and input into my work including Jeremy Ward, Mark Godliman, Mike Cawthorn, Andy Wilkinson, Dave Grayson, Kieran Eblett, Dan Homer, Bruce Carnegie-Brown, Mark Preston, Sir Laurie Magnus and Graham Bird. I'd also like to thank Susannah Schofield who got me started on this originally, Emily Bedford for agreeing to publish my book, Allie Collins and the rest of team at Bloomsbury and in particular Matt James who pushed me constantly to make sure I finished this (thanks Matt!)

I'd like to thank Duncan Parkes for getting me excited about private equity all those years ago and patiently explaining how you create value in businesses. Likewise Ashley Bragg for his support and guidance in all things technology related – both early in my career and as an ongoing sounding board. I'd like to thank my folks, David and Eleanor, for their advice, support, proofreading and encouragement and last (but not least), I'd like to thank my long-suffering wife Nicola and our two children Rowan and Imogen, who put up with me locking myself away in my study for months on end in order to finish this book.

INDEX

advertising   51, 59–60,
  72–3, 78, 102
AI-based systems   116,
  121–2, 123, 125,
  129–31, 133, 153–4
algorithms, search
  engine 61
application programming
  interfaces (APIs)
  139, 193
apps as product   93–6
artificial intelligence (AI)
  see AI-based systems
automation, marketing
  67, 72–86, 89

billing and invoicing
  165, 169
bills of materials (BOMs)
  157–8
built-in customer service
  processes   41, 47
business intelligence (BI)
  tools   135–9
  AI-based predictive
  analytics service
  153–4
  case studies   151–4
  data quality and matching
  146–8, 155
  database/data warehouse
  141–2, 149
  dealing with historic
  data   148–9
  employing expertise
  141, 150, 155
  extract and transfor-
  mation tools (ETL)
  140–1, 147, 149
  fixing untrustworthy
  data   147–9

front-end BI reporting
  tools   142–4
  mobile-friendly
  options   151
  proof of concepts
  tools   150
  raw data sources   139,
  155
  start small and
  build   149–50
  statistical functions
  144, 151
  understanding the
  questions that need
  asking   144–6
  understanding tool
  strengths   150–1, 155
business process
  management (BPM),
  digitizing   113–14
  AI-based systems   116,
  121–2, 123, 125,
  129–31, 133
  application forms
  114–15, 118–19
  business rules/
  decision engine
  component   117
  case study   131–2
  choosing the right
  processes   124–5
  coding systems   126
  customer facing
  114–15, 132
  customer service
  systems 115
  doing the work humans
  undertake   120–2,
  124, 132
  employing expertise
  121, 133

form design/data
  capture component
  116–17
  getting employees
  on board - starting
  small   126–7
  improving cost and
  efficiency   122–4, 133
  improving work that
  humans undertake
  118–20, 123–4, 132
  integrating new and old
  systems   127–8
  internally   115–16
  large systems   118–19,
  132
  limiting human to RPA
  handoffs   126, 133
  low code systems
  119–20, 132
  process designer
  component 116
  report production
  component 118
  robotic process
  automation (RPA)
  116, 117, 118, 120–1,
  123, 124, 125, 126,
  127–9, 133
  understanding
  limitations   128–9
  workflow/execution
  components   117–18
business strategy   21–5,
  238, 242
  cash improvement
  and technology
  strategy   24, 26
  professionalization
  and technology
  strategy   24, 26

sales and technology
strategy 25–6
steering IT Managers
27–9

call pooling 38, 45
'call to action' points,
website 58
cash generation and ERP
systems 164–5
cash improvement
strategy 24, 26
chatbots 130
Cloud computing
case study 195–6
concept overview
179–83
connectivity 191, 197
creating value 187–94
financial impact
187–91, 196–7
flexibility 184
geographic considerations
194, 197
hybrid cloud environ-
ment 185–6, 196
infrastructure as a service
(IAAS) 186, 192
platform as a service
(PAAS) 186
private cloud providers
184–5, 186, 196
public cloud providers
183–4, 185–6, 191, 196
round the clock access
requirements 193–4
security 184, 185
software as a service
(SAAS) 187, 192–3,
197
specialist support
194–5
coding BPM systems
126
collaboration technology
availability of infor-
mation 209–10
business culture
211–13, 217

case study 214–16
complexity of setting
up 213
document collaboration
203
identifying objectives
208–10
instant messaging and
social media 207–8
internal and external
use of 210–11
knowledge-management
tools 205, 209–10
multi-location business
practice 208–9,
214–16
non-real-time
collaboration 202–5
overview 199–202
privacy and security
issues 213–14
project or task
collaboration 203–5
real-time collaboration
206–8, 216
time and diary manage-
ment 205–6
video conferencing
206–7, 216
whiteboarding 206, 216
workplace flexibility
201–2
communication history
monitoring 41
comparable transactions
6–11, 14
competitive sales
culture 46
competitors, identifying
39
connectivity and Cloud
computing 191–2,
197
consistency, driving 36
contact forms 64, 71
contact information
management
39–40
Covid-19 200–1

customer buying
process 52–4, 65
customer facing processes
114–15, 132
customer feedback 67–71
customer relationship
management (CRM)
systems 25–6, 33,
34–5
built-in customer
service processes
41, 47
case study 46–7
communication
history 41
contact information
39–40
customer purchase
information 40–1
integration with other
systems 63–4, 78,
82, 83–4
managing implemen-
tation 42–4, 48
managing staff
limitations 42–4
purpose of 34
quantifying relationship
value 40
customer service processes
41, 47, 105–6, 110, 115

dashboard/chart
creation see business
intelligence (BI) tools
data-capture forms 78,
116–17
data capture, systemized
45–6, 116–17
data cleansing 146–7,
148–9, 171–2
data format 146–7
data quality 102–3, 109,
120, 128, 146–8, 155,
169–70
data science services 71,
136, 155
data security 104–5,
110

databases/data warehouses
70–1, 73–4, 97, 141–2
see also insight and
analytics tools
deal amount rules   36
debtors, chasing   169
decision engines/business
rule, BMP and   117
digital design companies
56–7
digital presence   49
digital video technology
99–100
digitizing process *see*
business process
management
discounted future cash-
flow model   15–18
document collaboration
203

EBIT   188, 190, 197
EBITA   7, 10, 11
EBITDA   7, 10, 11,
188–90, 197
email marketing and
tracking   75–6, 87–8
Enterprise Resource
Planning (ERP)
systems   157–60
benefits of training
first   173–4, 178
billing, invoicing,
debtors   165, 169
case studies   175–7
data cleansing - what data
do you need?   171–2,
177–8
data quality   169–70
employing expertise
175–6
impact on value
chain   164–6
implementing
incrementally   174
integration with
hardware   163
inter-departmental
collaboration   174–5,
178

inventory control
164–5, 168
potential implementation
difficulties   165–6
process review
opportunity   172
purpose of   160–1, 177
typical functions   162
understanding your real
objective   166–9, 177
enterprise value/revenue
metrics   11, 13
enterprise value/sales
ratio metrics   9
environmental, social
governance (ESG)   29
extensions and integrations,
website   63–4
extract and transformation
tools (ETL)   140–1,
147

feedback, customer
67–71
finance systems   26,
28–9, 165, 169
front-end BI reporting
tools   142–4

GDPR   194, 212–13, 214
geo-data/location
information   78, 151
global pandemic
(2020)   200–1

human resource (HR)
management   168–9

information/data,
monetizing   96–7,
102–3, 106–9
Infrastructure as a Service
(IAAS)   186, 192
insight and analytics
tools   73–5, 77–8,
87, 88
instant messaging
207–8
Internet of things
(IoT)   98

inventory control   26,
164–5, 168
IT managers and business
strategy   27–9

joint ventures   104

key words/search
terms   62
knowledge-management
systems   205, 209–10

landing pages   78, 82–3
lead scoring   77, 84–5
lead time tracking   36, 37
leads becoming opportu-
nities   38–9, 45, 48
low code systems   119–20

machine learning systems
130–1, 133
marketing technology
67
automation platforms
67, 72–86, 89
campaign feedback
72–3
case studies   86–8
collecting vs buying
data   81
customer feedback   67
email marketing and
tracking   75–6, 87–8
geo-data   78
identifying realistic
goals   78–81
inbound   73
insight and analytics
tools   73–5, 77–8,
87, 88
lead scoring   77, 84–5
personalizing content
82
proprietary databases
70–1
social-listening tools
68–71, 88
social media   69–71,
73, 76–7
system integration   83–

targeting customers
67, 72–5, 81–2
working with your sales
team   85–6
Material Requirements
Planning (MRP)
157–8
metadata, website   62–3
multiple, valuation
7–10, 11

natural language processing
(NLP)   70, 129
non-real-time collaboration
technologies   202–6

online courses, monetizing
97–8
online services   99–100
operational earnings,
measuring   7
opportunities from
leads   38–9

paper-free offices   29
pay-per-click advertising
(PPC)   51, 59–60,
66, 82–3
PBT   188
performance management
systems   26
performance monitoring
37, 38, 39, 46
pipeline management
36–7, 45, 47
Platform as a Service
(PAAS)   186
plugins, website   63
price to earnings ratio
11, 13
process change impact
39
process management
software (BPM)   113
process review   172
Professional Services
Automation (PSA)
systems   157–60
benefits of training
first   173–4, 178

data cleansing - what data
do you need?   171–2,
177–8
data quality   169–70
impact on value
chain   164–6
implementing
incrementally   174
inter-departmental
collaboration   174–5,
178
process review
opportunity   172
purpose of   160–1
resource management
165
typical functions   162–3
understanding your real
objective   166–9, 177
professionalization
strategy   24, 26
profit growth   24
business intelligence
tools   135–55
collaboration technology
199–217
Cloud computing
179–97
cost and efficiency
saving   111–12
digitizing process
113–33
ERP and PSA systems
156–78
project management
219–20, 243
agile - Scrum   230–7,
239–40
building   226–7
documentation
229–30
estimating timeframe
233–5
implementation/going
live   228–9
investment appraisal
237–40
iterative methodologies
220, 221–2, 230–7,
239–40

people and governance
229–30
problem identification
223, 230
product backlog   230–3
product owners   236
project design   226
requirements gathering
223–6
Scrum masters   236
sequential methodologies
220–1, 222–9
sprints/sprint planning
meetings   235–7, 239
technical testing   227,
228
testing stages   227–8
user testing   227–8
waterfall project manage-
ment   222–9, 238
project/task collaboration
203–5
proof of concepts tools
150
proprietary databases
70–1, 73–4, 97

raw data sources   139, 155
real-time collaboration
206–8, 216
recommender systems
130
reducing headcount
120–2, 124
requirement documents,
approaching   223–6
revenue growth   24
marketing insight and
automation   67–89
salesforce management
and CRM   33–48
technology as product
91–110
website and digital
presence   49–66
review sites   71
Robotic Process Automa-
tion (RPA) tools   116,
117, 118, 120–1, 123,
124, 125, 126, 127–9, 133

sales engine management
37–9, 48
salesforce management
systems 33–6
case study 44–6
managing implemen-
tation 48
pipeline management
36–7, 45, 47
sales engine management
37–9, 48
tracking leads to
opportunities 38–9,
45, 48
website integration
63–4
search engine optimisation
(SEO) 51, 59–63,
66, 77
server technology 27
shopping cart
abandonment
plugins 63
smart website
development 25
social-listening tools
68–71, 88
social media 69–71, 73,
76–7, 207–8
software and apps,
monetizing 93–6
Software as a Service
(SAAS) 187, 192–3,
197
staff limitations 42–4, 48
system integration tools,
RPA as 127–8

targeting customers 67,
72–5, 81–2
technical strategy
and business
alignment 21–9
technology as product
91–3

bringing in expertise
103–4
case study 106–9
customer service
and support
considerations
105–6, 110
data quality and
security 102–3,
109, 110
development
methodology
105, 110
identifying what's
possible 100
identifying where
your value will come
from 100–2, 109
information and
data 96–7, 102–3,
104–5, 106–9
joint venture 104
online courses 97–8
online services 99–100
physical goods and
digital support 95, 98
software and apps
93–6
technical infrastructure
104–5, 110
telephone systems 38, 45

valuation multiple 7–10,
13, 24
value, measuring 5–6,
18–19, 242
comparable company
analysis (CCA)
approach 11–13
comparable transactions
6–11, 14
discounted future cash-
flow model 15–18
video conferencing
206–7

video technology, digital
99–100
virtual assistants 130
virtual reality (VR) 207

warehouse management
systems 26
waterfall project
management 222–9,
238
website development 25,
49
call to action points 58
case study 64–5
contact forms 64, 71
content 58–9
customer buying
process 52–4, 65
digital design
companies 56–7
extensions and
integrations 63–4
intelligent and informed
design 54–8, 65–6
invisible aspects 62–3
key words and search
terms 62–3
navigability 51
pay-per-click advertising
(PPC) 51, 59–60, 66
search engine
optimisation (SEO)
51, 59–63, 66
understanding search
engines 60–2
user-experience
testing 57, 62
visual aspects 50, 62
website as level playing
field 51, 56, 65
website review sites 71
whiteboarding 206,
216
workplace flexibility
201–2